OUT OF THIS WORLD

OUT OF THIS WORLD

Science Fiction: but not as you know it

Mike Ashley

THE BRITISH LIBRARY

First published 2011 by
The British Library
96 Euston Road
London NW1 2DB

On the occasion of the exhibition at the
British Library
'Out of This World: Science Fiction but not
as you know it'
25 May – 25 September 2011
This exhibition has been made possible by the
provision of insurance through the Government
Indemnity Scheme. The British Library would like
to thank the Department for Culture, Media and
Sport for providing and arranging this indemnity.

The British Library acknowledges with
gratitude the financial assistance of the Friends
and Patrons of the British Library towards this
exhibition.

ISBN 978 0712 5835 4 (paperback)
ISBN 978 07123 5831 6 (hardback)

Designed and typeset by Andrew Shoolbred
Colour reproductions by Dot Gradations
Printed and bound in Hong Kong by Great Wall
Printing Co. Ltd

Half-title image
Wood engraving from *L'Atmosphère: meteorology
populaire* (1888) by Camille Flammarion. Symbolic
of a conceptual breakthrough, the image shows a
medieval missionary discovering the point where
the Earth and the sky meet.
8755.k13.p.163

Frontispiece image
Painting by Edward Miller for *Perdido Street Station* by
China Miéville (2010 edition).

Acknowledgements
The author is grateful to the following for their
help and advice:

Slaney Begley, Janet Benoy, Catherine Britton,
Damien Broderick, John Clute, Dennis Lien, Sally
Nicholls, David Pringle, Ekaterina Rogatchevskaia,
Andy Sawyer and Endre Zsoldos.

Picture acknowledgements
a = above, **b** = below, **r** = right, **l** = left

2, 95 Edward Miller; **5, 25l, 76–77** UFA/The
Kobal Collection; **6, 32b, 45, 60, 69, 89b, 91,
94, 115, 119l** Used with permission of the
Frank R. Paul Estate; **7, 8–9, 22, 23a** NASA;
18 Science Museum/Science & Society Picture
Library; **20** NY Daily News via Getty Images;
25r Mezhrabpom/The Kobal Collection;
26 Rocket Publishing/SSPL/Getty Images; **27**
Copyright © 1964 by Dell Magazines; **28, 29,
38, 39b, 60l, 69, 72, 73** Private Collection;
29 Copyright © 1962 by Dell Magazines;
32 Copyright © 1970 by Dell Magazines; **33**
Copyright © 1960 by Street & Smith Publications,
Inc., reprinted by permission of Dell Magazines;
33r, 54, 61 Used with permission of The
Magazine of Fantasy and Science Fiction; **34**
Archives du 7e Art/DR/Photo 12; **35** Copyright
© 1945 by Street & Smith Publications, Inc.,
reprinted by permission of Dell Magazines; **36r,
39a** Copyright © 1994 by Dell Magazines; **37**
Copyright © 1965 by Dell Magazines; **40** Enki
Balal © Casterman S.A.; **42** © David A. Hardy/
www.astroart.org, from the private collection
of Mr Richard Haynes; **46** © 19**, J.G. Ballard.
Reproduced by permission. All rights reserved.;
47, 56 Used with permission of Interzone;
48 Universal/The Kobal Collection; **50–51**
The Estate of Frederick Siebel; **52r** Copyright
© 1941 by Street & Smith Publications, Inc.,
reprinted by permission of Dell Magazines;
53 BBC Worldwide; **57** From *League of Extraordinary
Gentlemen* © DC Comics; **59, 104, 113l, 122,**
131, 135r Collection of John Clute; **60r, 133**
Mary Evans Picture Library; **62-63** Warner
Bros/The Kobal Collection; **65** © Luigi Serafini;
74 National Theatre Archive; **79, 80–81** British
Museum; **91l, 106–107** University of Liverpool
Library; **92** Ladd Company/Warner Bros/The
Kobal Collection; **99** Copyright © 1992 by Dell
Magazines; **100** Marvel Enterprises/The Kobal
Collection; **102** Copyright © 1986 by Dell
Magazines; **103** 20th Century Fox/The Kobal
Collection; **105** Science Photo Library; **108** ©
Dougal Dixon; **110–111, 117** © David A. Hardy/
www.astroart.org; **114** Allied Artists/The Kobal
Collection; **119r** Copyright © 1988 by Dell
Magazines; **120** Hawk Films Prod/Columbia/The
Kobal Collection; **123** Reproduced by permission
of Penguin Books Ltd.; **132** Cinecom/Bioskop/
Cinetudes/The Kobal Collection; **136, 137r**
Columbia/The Kobal Collection

Note

All book, film and magazine titles are shown in
italics. Short story and essay titles are shown in
'single quotes'. For non-English books, if the book
has been translated into English its title is given
in brackets in italics, followed by the original
publication date. For example, if translated:

Jules Verne, *Vingt Mille Lieues sous les mers* (20,000
Leagues Under the Sea, 1870)

If a title has not been translated (trans.) the title
is shown in brackets, but not in italics:

Vasilii Levshin, *Viaje de un Filósofo a Selenópolis*
(Voyage of a Philosopher to Selenopolis, 1804)

Contents

Introduction

We live in a science-fiction world. We take for granted items that were the dreams of a few visionaries only a generation or two ago – personal computers, organ transplants, mobile phones, space travel, virtual reality – all of which have enhanced and improved our lives.

The pace of change continues to accelerate at an increasingly rapid rate. Some scientists have suggested that we are reaching the point they call the technological singularity, where change is so fast that it goes beyond human understanding.

We have also become aware of the potential harm such progress may cause. Climate change, nuclear destruction, social upheaval, genetic engineering – all these things and more have caused widespread public concern in the last few decades.

Except, of course, in the world of science fiction, which has considered these matters for far longer. When the first atom bomb was detonated in 1945 it was said that the only people not surprised were science-fiction fans.

For many years science fiction was considered a minority market for a rather freakish readership, but today it is arguably the most popular of all fields of fiction. The majority of the highest-grossing films of all time are science fiction or fantasy. TV series such as *Dr Who* and *Star Trek* have become part of our culture. Science-fiction books are frequently amongst the bestsellers with some, such as George Orwell's *Nineteen Eighty-Four*, amongst the bestselling books of all time.

Some of you may pause at this point and say, 'Hang on. *Nineteen Eighty-Four* isn't science fiction.' Isn't it? Why not? What about other books such as Aldous Huxley's *Brave New World*, Len Deighton's *SS-GB* or Margaret Atwood's *The Handmaid's Tale*? Are these science fiction?

Whether they are or not depends on the definition of science fiction. There is often a narrow perception that science fiction is primarily for a juvenile readership and concentrates on adventures in time and space. Even when the tropes of science fiction are used in literary works some will argue that this does not make those works science fiction. It is a selective judgement that means that science fiction tends to be judged by its worst examples, whilst its best examples are redefined as 'literature'.

The term, as it is used today, was coined by Hugo Gernsback in 1929, who defined it simply as 'a charming romance intermingled with scientific fact and prophetic vision'. Gernsback wanted to use science fiction as a medium to raise people's awareness of the potential of science whilst also entertaining them. It can still do that, but as the field has developed writers have found it can do so much more, by way of social commentary and studying the human condition in unusual circumstances.

One of the purposes of this book is to demonstrate the scope of science fiction. It has been called the literature of ideas or the literature of change, but above all it is the literature of 'otherness'. It is by confronting this 'otherness', such as space travel or alien invasion or new technology, that writers can hold a mirror up to ourselves and society and show how we react. Science fiction is that speculation about the impact of science, technology and socio-political change on us, hence the alternative phrase 'speculative fiction'.

Right Galileo's *Sidereus Nuncius* (1653 edition), showing one of his drawings of the surface of the Moon. When first published in 1610 his book revolutionized thought about the Moon and beyond, and turned minds towards speculation and, in time, science fiction.
1484.cc.23

Far right *Amazing Stories*, April 1928. A symbolic cover by Frank R. Paul, depicting the 'Age of Progress', showing how technology has raised humanity from its Stone Age origins to the present day.
PP.6383.ccs

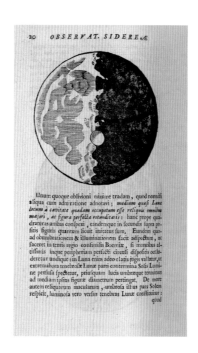

The launch of *Viking 1* from Cape Canaveral, 20 August 1975. This was the first spacecraft to land successfully on Mars and remained in operation for six years.

The field has an ancient pedigree, dating back, in Western cultures, at least as far as the ancient Greeks. Although it may seem primarily a British and American phenomenon, science fiction is international and examples can be found in all the major countries of the world. The roots of science fiction found fertile soil in France, Germany and Russia at least as early, if not earlier, than it did in Britain or the United States.

This book which accompanies British Library's exhibition on science fiction, *Out of This World: Science Fiction but not as you know it*, looks at the origins, nature and scope of science fiction through six primary themes: Alien Worlds, Time and Parallel Worlds, Virtual Worlds, Future Worlds, the End of the World and Perfect Worlds. It is impossible in a book of this size to cover the subject in detail, and the emphasis is on the unusual and unexpected. Nevertheless, it will cover many key books and authors, and raise a number of moral, ethical and social questions. There are some surprises in store. It is all science fiction – but not necessarily as you know it!

Alien Worlds

One of the oldest questions must be 'What's out there?'

To the ancients, this question would have arisen not only from staring at the night sky, but also wondering what lay beyond the forests, mountains and oceans. As our ability to travel improved, so did our awareness of the rich diversity of our world.

Some of the earliest stories that classify as science fiction are travellers' tales with their exaggerations of strange beasts and fabled lands. The journey taken by Odysseus and his men returning home from the Trojan War, retold in the epic poem the *Odyssey* attributed to Homer (seventh or eighth century BC), is one of the earliest imaginary voyages and its offspring can be seen to the present day via *Gulliver's Travels* and the novels of Jules Verne.

In a similar vein are the stories about Sinbad the Sailor, known from the *Arabian Nights*, of Persian origin (*Hazār Afsān*, A Thousand Tales, ninth century), drawing upon Arab and Indian folklore. Like Odysseus, Sinbad used his cunning to outwit both human and supernatural foes, showing rational traits rather than superstitious ones.

The desire to explore led humans to populate the globe, and that drive has never left us. Future generations will undoubtedly leave the Earth and colonize other worlds. Perhaps we will discover other life forms – or perhaps they will discover us.

Encountering strange life forms and alien cultures was just as much a part of the early travellers' tales as it is a part of science fiction today, and the fear that there may be aliens out there, watching us, has given rise to the belief in UFOs and alien 'cover-ups'. Maybe the aliens are already amongst us – or are we alone in the universe?

Until the late sixteenth century no one imagined other intelligent life forms. It would have been considered heresy. The philosopher and astronomer Giordano Bruno was burned at the stake (in 1600) for, amongst other things, promoting the idea of other populated worlds, the 'plurality of worlds' as it was known, in his book *De l'infinito universo et mondi* (*On the Infinite Universe and Worlds*, 1584).

Now we believe the opposite. In 1950 the Italian physicist Enrico Fermi wondered why, given the vast number of stars in the universe and the probability of countless planets, we have found no evidence of extraterrestrial life. In 1960 Frank Drake established SETI (Search for Extraterrestrial Intelligence), now part of the SETI Institute, which has developed a series of initiatives searching for any evidence of life.

The exploration of space, the study of other worlds (both on, in and beyond the Earth), the search for alien life forms, and how we would recognize and communicate with aliens has been a staple diet of science fiction from earliest times and is the focus of this section.

Right A montage of images taken by the *Voyager 1* spacecraft of the planets and four of Jupiter's moons. (NASA)

Inset The *Voyager 1* spacecraft, launched on 5 September 1977 and now the most remote human-made object, at over 17 billion km from the Sun.

Voyages Extraordinaires

The expression 'voyages extraordinaires' was used by the French publisher Jules Hetzel to brand the scientific adventure novels of Jules Verne, such as *Twenty Thousand Leagues Under the Sea* (1870) and *Around the World in Eighty Days* (1873). Verne's work, though, was a continuation of the fantastic voyage story that had been around for over two thousand years.

At the height of the Roman Empire, stories of imaginary voyages were all the rage, but few have survived. The great wit of the age, Lucian of Samosata, parodied them in *Alēthēs historia* (*True History*, c.170AD). He chastised those who believed such tales and emphasized that his story was all lies. His travellers pass through the Pillars of Hercules into the Atlantic Ocean and visit various islands before being caught in a storm and carried to the Moon on a giant waterspout. On their return, they are swallowed by an enormous whale inside of which is a city built by previous victims, and they visit the Isles of the Blessed, a paradise for the dead.

The passion for travellers' tales was rekindled by Marco Polo's accounts of his travels through the Middle East and Central Asia to the court of Kublai Khan. Polo dictated them to the writer Rustichello da Pisa in about 1298–9, and they appeared under the title *Livres des merveilles du monde* (*Books of the Marvels of the World*). Few believed the account at the time and there remain doubts over its full authenticity. Another who exaggerated his adventures was John de Mandeville (an alias, probably for Jean de Bourgogne, a physician in Liège) who claimed to have travelled as far as Cathay. In his *Travels* (completed c.1370) he describes Amazonia, the land of women, and inhabitants of the isles of the East Indies including one-eyed giants, people with horse's hooves and others with no heads but eyes in their shoulders.

Regardless of their veracity, accounts by Polo and Mandeville inspired Christopher Columbus to find a new route to the Orient. His discovery of the Americas in 1492, and the circumnavigation of

the world by Ferdinand Magellan's crew in 1522, encouraged further explorers' tales. This period also saw the emergence of accounts of utopian lands, such as Thomas More's *Utopia* (1516), Tommaso Campanella's *Civitas Solis* (*The City of the Sun*, 1623) and Francis Bacon's *New Atlantis* (1624).

The definitive traveller's tale, though, and one of the most influential imaginary voyages, was *Gulliver's Travels* (1726) by Jonathan Swift. Besides satirizing the politics of Britain and Ireland, the book ridicules human nature and its ability to create problems rather than solutions. Satire is a fundamental element of science

Left *Niels Klims underjordiske Reise (Niels Klim's Underground Journey)* by Ludvig Holberg from the 1789 Copenhagen edition, depicting the tree people of Nazar.
89.g.3

Right *Travels* of Sir John Mandeville, depicting some of the fantastic creatures he describes. Taken from the German 1482 edition *Itinerarium*.
G.6774

Below Laputa as depicted by J. J. Grandville from the 1838 Paris edition of Jonathan Swift's *Gulliver's Travels*.
838.f.24

Item do ist ein andere insel do seind auch gar vnsauber vnd scheützlich leüt jnnen dyeselbi geu dye haben auch nicht haub ter vmd es steen in die augen an iren achseln. So steet jnen auch der mundt mitten an der prust vmd ist jnen krums auf ein seyten gericht als ein hüff eysen damit man die pferdt be schlecht auch so haben diesel bigen leüt in derselbigen inseln gar grosse vnnd vnd auch wei te augen

Hye merckt von wunderlichen leüten den ist das antlutz flach als ein teler

Item aber so ist ein ander in seln jn derselben do seind auch leüte den ist das antlueze aller ding gantz vmd gar flach alls ein teler vmd haben auch kei nen mund dann an der stat do in der mund sol steen do haben sy zwey kleine löchlin vnd sy sein auch auß dermassen vast zornig

In d
die hab
vnnd

wenn sy an der sunnen ligen

Jonathan Swift (1667–1745)

Irish-born writer and dean of St Patrick's Cathedral, Dublin, author of *Gulliver's Travels*, first published as *Travels Into Several Remote Nations of the World* (1726). The book recounts Gulliver's voyages to Lilliput, where everyone is one-twelfth human size; Brobdingnag, where giants are twelve times human size; the flying island of Laputa occupied by mad scientists; and the land of intelligent horses, the Houyhnhnms, and ignorant humanoids, the Yahoos. Within his biting satire Swift made several important social and scientific observations. The immortal Struldbrugs allowed him to comment upon the perils of longevity without equal improvements in health. He favoured the Lilliputian idea of removing children from their parents and having them reared by the State, and he proposed population control seventy years ahead of Thomas Robert Malthus, with the Houyhnhnms having just one child of each sex. He also stated that Mars had two moons, which was not established for another 150 years.

fiction, exploring as it does the differences between our society and others. Swift, living in what became known as the Age of Enlightenment, was pessimistic about social and scientific progress and showed, in the episode in Laputa, how scientists divorced themselves from society, and worked more for their own benefit than their countrymen.

The novel that made the move from satire to adventure and introduced the lost-race theme was *The Life and Adventures of Peter Wilkins* (1751) by Robert Paltock. Wilkins is shipwrecked near the Antarctic and is washed through a subterranean cavern to a hidden land. He rescues a flying woman and helps her family in their battle against a rival race. The book's popularity grew

slowly and was praised by Samuel Taylor Coleridge, influencing his own imaginary voyage, *The Rime of the Ancient Mariner* (1798).

Perhaps the most extreme of travellers' tales was *Baron Münchausen's Narrative of his Marvellous Travels* (1785), compiled anonymously by Rudolf Erich Raspe from stories serialized in Germany in 1781–3 and embellished by others over the next few decades. Baron Münchhausen was a Prussian cavalry officer renowned for his 'tall tales', such as a journey to the Moon by ship in a whirlwind, a flight on a cannonball and a journey through the Earth to the South Seas. Whilst more fantasy than science fiction, these tales encouraged later writers to exaggerate the potential of science for effect. They were

Jules Verne's favourite childhood reading, whilst Hugo Gernsback, who coined the term science fiction, wrote his own escapade, 'The Scientific Adventures of Baron Münchausen' in 1915.

The late Victorian fascination for explorers' tales and lost worlds encouraged the fantastic adventure story, starting with *She* (1887) by H. Rider Haggard, set in the depths of the African continent. In *The Lost World* (1912) Arthur Conan Doyle placed his isolated land of dinosaurs on an inaccessible mountain in South America. Edgar Rice Burroughs set his similar lost world on a tropically heated island near Antarctica in *The Land That Time Forgot* (1918; book, 1924). One of the last of the lost-world novels, James Hilton's *Lost Horizon*

Jules Verne (1828–1905)

French novelist, the most prolific writer of scientific adventure stories of
his day, and the first popular writer of science fiction. He may well be
the bestselling science-fiction writer of all time. After the success of his
first book, *Cinq semaines en ballon* (*Five Weeks in a Balloon*, 1863),
in which three intrepid adventurers attempt to explore darkest Africa
by balloon, his publisher, Jules Hetzel, encouraged him to write similar
adventure stories, rejecting his futuristic speculative novel *Paris au
XXᵉ siècle* (*Paris in the 20th Century*), which remained unpublished
until 1994. Verne concentrated on stories that explored the potential
of new or proposed inventions out of which he could create such
visionary adventures that he inspired many generations of writers
and would-be scientists. The young Hermann Oberth, for example,
was so overwhelmed by Verne's *De la Terre à la Lune* (*From the Earth
to the Moon*, 1865) that he spent his life pioneering rocket science.
Verne's best known *voyages extraordinaires* include *Voyage au
centre de la Terre* (*Journey to the Centre of the Earth*, 1864), *Vingt
mille lieues sous les mers* (*Twenty Thousand Leagues Under the
Sea*, 1870), *Le Tour du monde en quatre-vingts jours* (*Around
the World in Eighty Days*, 1873), and *Robur-le-Conquérant*
(also known as *The Clipper of the Clouds*, 1886). Amongst
his lesser-known books, *Le Sphinx des glaces* (*The Sphinx of
the Ice Fields*, 1897, also known as *An Antarctic Mystery*)
was a sequel to Edgar Allan Poe's *The Narrative of Arthur
Gordon Pym*. Poe had inspired Verne just as Verne inspired
thousands, showing that science fiction grew and prospered
with each generation.

(1933), depicts the paradise of Shangri-
La tucked away in a remote valley in the
Himalayas.

As voyages of discovery mapped the
globe there became fewer locales for lost
lands, so some writers went underground.
As long ago as 1665 in *Mundus Subterraneus*,
Athanasius Kircher had described an
Earth riddled with tunnels, not unlike
those explored in Jules Verne's *Journey to the
Centre of the Earth* (1864), with its central
sea and prehistoric monsters. Inspired
by *Gulliver's Travels*, the Danish-Norwegian
writer Ludvig Holberg created a mini solar
system within the Earth in *Nicolai Klimii iter
subterraneum* (*Niels Klim's Underground Journey*,
1741). His hero falls through a hole into
the Earth and finds himself in orbit around

a central sun and the planet Nazar. He uses
the creatures and cultures he encounters
to satirize life in his homeland.

In 1818, the US army officer John
Cleves Symmes, Jr proposed that the Earth
was hollow with cavernous openings
at both poles. His ideas inspired many
books, such as *Symzonia* (1820) by the
pseudonymous Adam Seaborn, Edgar Allan
Poe's *The Narrative of Arthur Gordon Pym of
Nantucket* (1838) and Mary E. Bradley Lane's
feminist utopia, *Mizora* (1881). Another
early work of interest set under the Earth
is *The Coming Race* (1871) by Edward
Bulwer Lytton, where a vastly superior
underground race derives its power from
an electromagnetic source called vril – a
term adopted for the beef-drink Bovril.

The subterranean tale still has life in it, as
shown by Jeff Long in *The Descent* (1999)
and sequels, which reveals a race of devil-
like creatures in deep caverns. Alternate
Earths provide further opportunities in
Circumpolar! (1984) by Richard A. Lupoff
and *The Hollow Earth* (1990) by Rudy Rucker.

The earthbound explorers' tale has
faded with global mapping, although the
lost world has not entirely vanished – as
shown by the success of the TV series
Lost (2004–10). But authors had already
looked long ago to space to continue the
voyage extraordinaires.

Fly Me to the Moon

In 1609 Galileo studied the heavens through his new telescope and recorded his findings in *Sidereus Nuncius* (*The Starry Messenger*, 1610). His description of the Moon as a distinct world with features similar to Earth's, rather than simply an orb, stimulated considerable interest. The playwright Ben Jonson incorporated Galileo's discoveries into his masque *News from the New World Discovered in the Moon* (1620).

The Ancient Greeks had believed that the Earth and the cosmos were all one world, so that it was easy to fly to the Moon through the atmosphere. In another of Lucian of Samosata's works, *Icaromenippus* (c.170 AD), the protagonist does just that by strapping an eagle's wing to one shoulder and a vulture's wing to the other. It was not until 1646 that Blaise Pascal demonstrated the atmosphere had an upper limit beyond which was a vacuum. Not everyone accepted his findings, however, and some scientists continued to believe space was filled with *aether* – a concept not disproved until 1887. A journey to the Moon was therefore not a question of space travel but of flight, and many and devious were the methods contrived.

Somnium, by the German astronomer Johannes Kepler, was written by 1609 but not published until 1634. Kepler drew on his own researches for his description of the lunar surface, but avoided the problem of travel by setting the story in a dream with the narrator transported by demons.

John Wilkins, the future brother-in-law of Oliver Cromwell and a keen promoter of scientific understanding, wrote *The Discovery of a World in the Moone* (1638, revised 1640) and *Mathematicall Magick* (1648), both of which considered whether the Moon might support life and how to reach it. Wilkins suggested three ways: a flying chariot, wings strapped to the body or conveyance by large birds. The last suggestion came from *The Man in the Moone* (1638, but written c.1628) by Francis Godwin, bishop of Hereford, who

has a good claim to writing the first work of science fiction in English. His hero, the diminutive Domingo Gonsales, trapped on St Helena, builds a harness to which he hooks several trained large geese or swans and is lifted off the island. To his surprise they fly to the Moon, where they overwinter.

Inspired by Godwin's book, Cyrano de Bergerac wrote *L'Autre Monde ou les États et Empires de la Lune* (1657) and *Les États et Empires du Soleil* (1662). Probably written in 1649–50, they are genuine science fiction as they sought to speculate on flight using the knowledge of the day.

Godwin's and Cyrano's works

influenced writers internationally. Britain's David Russen developed Cyrano's ideas by using a giant spring in *Iter Lunare* (1703). In *The Consolidator* (1705), Daniel Defoe has a machine that flies with feathered wings powered by a form of combustion engine. In *Noveishee puteshestvie, sochenennoe v gorode Beleve* (The Most Recent Journey that Happened in the Town of Belev, 1784), Russia's Vasilii Levshin has his hero fly to the Moon in a machine that consists of four eagle wings and a steering stick. *Viaje de un Filósofo a Selenópolis* (Voyage of a Philosopher to Selenopolis, 1804), believed to be by António Marqués y Espejo, is Spain's first science-fiction novel of a lunar society,

with a scientist taken there in a flexible ship with a huge sail and oars like fans.

Germany's Eberhard Kindermann has the first balloon journey to Mars in *Die geschwinde Reise auf dem Luft-Schiff nach der Oberen Welt* (Rapid Journey by Airship to the Upper World, 1744). Holland's Willem Bilderdijk took a short cut in *Kort verhall van eene aanmerklijke luchtreis en nieuwe planeetontdekking* (*A Short Account of a Remarkable Aerial Voyage and a Discovery of a New Planet*, 1813) and sent his traveller by balloon to a planet within the Earth's atmosphere halfway to the Moon.

A Voyage to the Moon (1827) by Joseph Atterley (pen name of American lawyer and historian, George Tucker) was the first novel to introduce the idea of an anti-gravity (or contra-terrene) material, here called lunarium. Anti-gravity became the primary 'scientific' travel device throughout the nineteenth century and was used by H.G. Wells in *The First Men in the Moon* (1901). No one seriously considered rocket propulsion, not even Jules Verne. In *From the Earth to the Moon* (1865) his travellers are fired from a huge cannon. In reality, the acceleration required to reach escape velocity within the barrel of a cannon would crush everyone to death. Even so, Wells still used this idea in his script for the film *Things to Come* (1936).

Savinien Cyrano de Bergerac (1619–55)

French soldier, noted for his swordsmanship, and the first author to use the idea of rocket-powered flight. His books, translated as *The Comical History of the States and Empires of the Worlds of the Moon and Sun* (1687), include not one but seven ways to leave the Earth. The narrator, Drycano, wishes to prove Galileo's assertion that the Moon is a distinct world. He straps bottles of water to his body, believing that as the water evaporates it will take him with it. It does, but not towards the Moon, so he returns to Earth. He builds a new contraption with spring-driven wings, which he launches from a cliff, but it crashes. To ease his bruises, he smothers himself in bone marrow. Meanwhile, soldiers steal his device and tie firework rockets to it so that it looks like a dragon. Drycano rescues the device, but is fired into the air by the rockets. When they burn out, Drycano finds he is drawn to the Moon by its attraction for marrow fat!

Seeking to reach the Sun, Drycano tries other methods. One is to stand on an iron plate and throw a strong magnet ever upwards! Another uses a sealed unit that draws in air, which is heated by mirrors and then expelled at the base – thus providing lift. (Arthur C. Clarke believed this was the first depiction of the ramjet principle.) A third is to build a globe that draws in smoke, causing the globe to rise. This was close to the idea of the hot-air balloon, which was not used in Europe for another 150 years.

Just imagine. The first manned hot-air balloon flight was recorded in 1783, though it has been speculated that the native culture in Peru may have achieved it over a thousand years earlier to design the figures on the Nazca plain. Suppose ancient cultures had travelled by hot-air balloon. Just how might that have changed history?

A montage depicting the early and varied attempts at space flight:

Far left Lucian of Samosata's travellers are carried to the Moon by ship in a storm in his *True History*, depicted here in *Lucian's Wonderland* (1899), illustrated by A. Payne Garnett.
12403.f.32

Left Francis Godwin's Domingo Gonsales trained a flock of ganzas to transport him in *The Man in the Moone*. From the first edition, 1638.
C.56.c.2

Below Cyrano de Bergerac described several ways of reaching the Moon. These two illustrations show his hero being fired aloft by rockets (from *Les Œuvres diverses de Monsieur Cyrano de Bergerac*, Amsterdam, 1699) and the rising globe, using the ramjet principle (from *The Comical History of the States and Empires of the Worlds of the Moon and Sun*, London, 1687).
012238.aa.2 (Vol.1) / 634.e.4

Right Jules Verne's space capsule being fired from a cannon in *From the Earth to the Moon*, from the 1876 Sampson, Low edition.
12511.ff.5

The Need to Believe

In 1686 Bernard de Fontenelle wrote in *Entretiens sur la pluralité des mondes* (*Conversations on the Plurality of Worlds*), 'Can you believe that after the earth has thus been made to abound with life, the rest of the planets have not a living creature in them?' Unlike Giordano Bruno, de Fontenelle was not burned at the stake. The dawn of the Age of Enlightenment in Europe meant people could ask such challenging questions. We are still asking this one today.

In 1794, William Herschel reluctantly accepted that the Moon probably did not have a breathable atmosphere. This marked the beginning of the end in the belief in an inhabited Moon. Herschel had discovered the first new planet, Uranus, in 1781 and was regarded as the greatest astronomer of his day. His reputation passed on to some extent to his son, John Herschel, which was why, in August 1835, thousands of readers of the New York Sun were duped by what became known as 'The Moon Hoax'. While Herschel was in South Africa plotting the night sky, the *Sun* announced that his powerful new telescope had found life on the Moon. Daily instalments referred to the flora, the animals and eventually people with enormous bat-like wings. Scientists and reporters converged on the Sun's offices for more details, and were referred to a Scottish-born reporter, Richard Adams Locke. He forestalled them but finally had to admit it was all a hoax. Herschel was unaware of this for months and was initially amused, but he grew increasingly irritated when people continued to question him about it. Like any good hoax, there are always those who are convinced it is true.

In *Orrin Lindsay's Plan of Aerial Navigation* (1847), Professor John Leonard Riddell produced another deception, albeit more scientific. He originally delivered the story as a series of lectures to his students, based, purportedly, on discussions with a former student who had developed a method of controlling gravity and had travelled to the Moon, but not landed. Science-fiction scholar Everett Bleiler called

Nouvelles découvertes dans la Lune,
Faites par Sir John Herschel dans son observatoire du cap de bonne espérance, d'après les dessins publiés par le journal des Sciences d'Edimbourg (Edinburg Journal of Sciences.)

it 'the first hard science-fiction story'. It is scientifically detailed (even if erroneous) and is significant as the first story to regard the Moon as lifeless.

The Moon as an abode of life took time to fade from science fiction. H.G. Wells's Selenites lived underground in *The First Men in the Moon* (1901), whilst Edmond Hamilton had them on the far side in 'The Other Side of the Moon' (1929). Otherwise the Moon has become the focal point for colonization (as in Arthur C. Clarke's *Prelude to Space*, 1951) or, more menacingly, as a base for aliens to monitor the Earth. This was memorably signified by the black monolith discovered there in Stanley Kubrick's film *2001: A Space Odyssey* (1968), scripted by Arthur C. Clarke from his short story 'Sentinel of Eternity' (1951). There is still a belief amongst ufologists in an alien base on the Moon.

Writers turned to Mars. Fontenelle had dismissed it in *Plurality of Worlds* as having 'nothing calculated to arrest

our attention'. So it remained, until 1877 when the Italian astronomer Giovanni Schiaparelli reported seeing a series of straight lines on the surface which he called *canali*, or 'channels'. This was mistranslated as 'canals'. The French astronomer Camille Flammarion conjectured in *La Planète Mars* (1892) that the canals were the work of an advanced civilization. The idea was further championed by the American astronomer Percival Lowell. He dismissed reports by fellow astronomers that they could see no canals and meticulously mapped them. He steadfastly stuck to his beliefs in his books *Mars* (1895), *Mars and Its Canals* (1906) and *Mars as the Abode of Life* (1908).

As a consequence, magazines of the period were filled with stories and features about life on Mars. There was a growing number of novels about trips to Mars. Percy Greg's *Across the Zodiac* (1880), the first to use the word 'astronaut', though as the name for the spaceship not the traveller,

Left 'Nouvelles Decouvertes dans la Lune'. A French print by the Thierry brothers depicting the inhabitants of the Moon as described in Richard Adams Locke's 'New Discoveries in the Moon' (1835).

Below and right A map of Schiaparelli's Martian canals and an artist's impression of a sunrise on Mars over the canals from Camille Flammarion's *Les Terres du Ciel* (1884).
8562.ff.17

was presented in a *faux* semi-factual frame as being a manuscript discovered among the wreckage of an extraterrestrial craft. In *Journey to Mars* (1894) by Gustavus W. Pope, another story presented as a manuscript found in a sealed box, there are three races of Martians: red, yellow and blue. This novel of a quasi-feudal Mars may have influenced Edgar Rice Burroughs's Martian series. In *Unveiling a Parallel* (1893), Alice Jones and Ella Merchant, writing as 'Two Women of the West', send a man to Mars by aeroplane and discover female superiority. Almost all these books depicted Martians as superior to humans, wise and benevolent.

So it came as a shock when Martians invaded the Earth in *The War of the Worlds* (1897) by H.G. Wells. Martians are portrayed as technologically advanced but hostile and ruthless. Wells showed how ill-prepared Britain was when facing an invader with superior technology, thus exploiting the fear of war that had been growing in Britain. Wells's Martians are only overcome when they succumb to terrestrial bacteria.

The War of the Worlds is probably Wells's best-known novel and a cornerstone of any science-fiction library, but it later became notorious. In 1938 Orson Welles broadcast a radio adaptation, heard across New York and New Jersey. The original had been updated and presented as a series of reality news stories. Listeners, not aware it was a drama, took the reports for real and a panic ensued. Although not intended as a hoax, the reaction to the broadcast, like that a century earlier for 'The Moon Hoax', showed the public's readiness to believe. That was the soil in which science fiction was taking root.

DAILY NEWS FINAL

Vol. 20. No. 109   New York, Monday, October 31, 1938   48 Pages   2 Cents

FAKE RADIO 'WAR' STIRS TERROR THROUGH U.S.

Story on Page 2

"War" Victim Caroline Cantlon, WPA actress, listening to this radio in West 49th St., heard announcement of "smoke in Times Square." Running to street, she fell, broke her arm.

"I Didn't Know". Orson Welles, after broadcast expresses amazement at public reaction. He adapted H. G. Wells' "War of the Worlds" for radio and played principal role. Left: a machine conceived for another H. G. Wells story. Dramatic description of landing of weird "machine from Mars" started last night's panic. —*Story on page 2.*

Above Report of the panic following Orson Welles's radio broadcast of *The War of the Worlds* in the New York *Daily News*, 31 October 1938.

Just imagine. You hear a report that a machine from space has landed somewhere near you, but nothing has happened yet and it may or may not be a hoax. What would you do?

Right The Martians from H.G. Wells's *The War of the Worlds*, as depicted by Alvim-Correa in the Belgian edition, *La Guerre des mondes* (1906).
L45/3317

Forgotten Visionaries

During the nineteenth century tales of space travel took on a greater degree of scientific rigour. Yet those who applied the rigour are not always the ones remembered.

In 1815 the British artist Edward Burney (cousin of writer Fanny Burney) drew a series of sketches, 'Q.Q. Esq.'s Journey to the Moon', which included the first proposal for a space suit. The hapless voyager did not make it to the Moon, but he did return to Earth by parachute. When Edgar Allan Poe took his eponymous hero to the Moon by balloon in 'Hans Phaal' (1835), he ensured there was an airtight compartment complete with an air condensor.

The credit for the first plausible suggestion for rocket propulsion (and the first scientific journey to Venus) goes to the French writer Achille Eyraud, who in *Voyage à Venus* (1865) described a spaceship with a reaction motor that is propelled by water. In *From the Earth to the Moon* (also 1865) Jules Verne launched his space capsule from Florida and on its return, in *Autour de la Lune* (*Around the Moon*, 1870), it lands in the sea and is recovered by ship – just as happened with the Apollo astronauts.

In 1869 the American Edward Everett Hale wrote 'The Brick Moon', the first story about an artificial satellite. The 'moon' consists of a series of small spheres within a larger sphere, 200 feet in diameter, and was intended as a navigational aid, but an accident launched

Above An artist's impression of Edward Everett Hale's 'The Brick Moon', first serialized in *Atlantic Monthly* in 1869.

Right The recovery of *Apollo 13* capsule on 17 April 1970 compared to the 1872 recovery of the space capsule in Jules Verne's *Autour de la lune* (Hetzel, 1872). 12514.I.20

Kurd Lasswitz (1848–1910)
German philosopher, scientist and teacher, noted for his history of science but best remembered today for his science fiction. During his lifetime his work was translated into most European languages except English, so he was virtually unknown to British and American readers. Yet his ideas were way ahead of his time. His first story, 'Bis zum Nullpunkt des Seins' (To the Absolute Zero of Existence, 1871), set in the year 2371, is a catalogue of inventions and social change including instant global news and opinion via public bulletin boards. Lasswitz suggested sleep-teaching machines, an idea favoured by Hugo Gernsback who launched the first science-fiction magazine, *Amazing Stories*, in 1926, and was clearly inspired by Lasswitz. Lasswitz's novel *Auf Zwei Planeten* (1897) fascinated a young Wernher von Braun who went on to create the German V2 rockets. He was also the brains behind the *Saturn V* rocket, which launched the first men to the Moon.

it prematurely, with people on board who survive and become self-sufficient. Although it seems bizarre that the satellite was launched from a giant flywheel and was built of brick, Hale undertook much research into the satellite's trajectory and feasibility. Fiction and scientific speculation were slowly coming together.

The two most significant authors to apply science to space travel were Kurd Lasswitz and Konstantin Tsiolkovsky. Lasswitz's *Auf Zwei Planeten* (1897) has only partially been translated into English (*Two Planets*, 1971). Explorers at the North Pole discover a colony of benign Martians, who are technically superior to humans. Needing water, the Martians want to trade with Earth and have established a space station positioned above the North Pole – the first reference to a space station in fiction. Lasswitz explores in detail the science behind the space station, the application of anti-gravity in space, and how to navigate between Mars and Earth.

At the time Lasswitz was writing in Germany, Konstantin Tsiolkovsky was exploring jet propulsion in Tsarist Russia. He was convinced it was the only way into space and had discussed it in a monograph, 'Svobodnoe prostranstvo' ('Free Space'), as early as 1883. His essay, 'Issledovanie mirovykh prostranst reaktivnymi priborami' ('The Exploration of Cosmic Space by Reaction-Propelled Apparatus'), detailed the principles of rocket design, but went unnoticed when the magazine in which the first part appeared in 1903 was banned by the secret police. It was not until 1911 that a new instalment caught the attention of aircraft pioneers. Tsiolkovsky had already turned to science fiction as a means to promote his ideas, describing the Moon in great detail in *Na lune* (*On the Moon*, 1887). Editors encouraged him to complete his novel *Vne Zemli* (*Outside the Earth*), which he had started in 1896. Part of it appeared in 1916 with the complete book in 1920. In it, an international team of scientists in a remote Himalayan castle unite to develop

E.F. Burney's depiction of the first space suit and rocket launch from his series of sketches 'Q.Q. Esq.'s Journey to the Moon' (1815). Reproduced from the *Illustrated London News*, 6 June 1959.
LON LD47 NPL

Below Konstantin Tsiolkovsky working on the design of his all-metal airship in 1933. From *The Call of the Cosmos* (Moscow, 1963).
11303.ff.1

Below right Tsiolkovsky's pamphlet, which translates as *The simplest project of a metal aeronaut made of corrugated iron* (1914), discusses the model airship he is constructing in the photograph.
C.114.r.7

a space rocket, which is tested in Earth's orbit before a flight to the Moon. It leads to the development of a space colonization programme.

Tsiolkovsky's work, unknown in Britain, was noted in Germany. The German rocket engineer Hermann Oberth, who had been inspired by reading Jules Verne as a child, and who had also considered the problems of space travel in *Die Rakete zu den Planetenräumen* (By Rocket into Planetary Space, 1923), acknowledged Tsiolkovsky's pioneering work. Oberth's design for a space rocket was used in Fritz Lang's film *Frau im Mond* (*Woman in the Moon*, 1929). Tsiolkovsky received a state pension from the Soviet government in 1921. He was a consultant on the first Soviet feature film about a Moon voyage, *Kosmicheskii reis* (*Cosmic Voyage*, 1936).

As with Lasswitz, none of Tsiolkovsky's work was available in English until the publication of *The Call of the Cosmos* in 1960. The same applied to Alexander Bogdanov's *Krasnaia zvezda* (*Red Star*, 1908). Written soon after the 1905 Russian revolution, it sought to portray an advanced socialist society on Mars, which includes a unisex approach between males and females. Although this novel was well known in Russia it was not translated into English until 1982, and then only in an abridged form.

Another pioneering author, the Polish Jerzy Żuławski, wrote a trilogy about the perils of exploring the Moon that still awaits an English translation.

Right Poster for Fritz Lang's 1929 film *Frau im Mond*, for which Hermann Oberth designed the space rocket.

Below A lobby card for the 1924 film *Aelita*. Like Lasswitz's novel, *Aelita* (1923) by Alexei Tolstoi depicted an advanced Martian civilization that is struggling to survive because of lack of water, when their irrigation system was ruined by civil war and social upheaval.

The first book, *Na Srebrnym Globie* (*On the Silver Globe*, 1901), tells of a disastrous expedition to the Moon in which most of the crew of two rocket-ships are killed and the survivors (two men and a woman) struggle for existence on the far side of the Moon. The sequels, *Zwycięzca* (*The Victor*, 1908) and *Stara Ziemia* (*Old Earth*, 1910), take place fifty years later. British and American science-fiction writers wanted to be positive about space exploration and only decades later did they consider the hazards of lunar exploration in Frank K. Kelly's 'The Moon Tragedy' (1933), John W. Campbell, Jr's *The Moon is Hell* (1951) and Arthur C. Clarke's *A Fall of Moondust* (1961).

It was also decades before the West learned of the works of Lasswitz, Tsiolkovsky, Bogdanov and Żuławski and accorded them due recognition.

When the French philosopher Voltaire wrote his satire *Micromégas* in 1752 he had no idea of the size of the universe, but knew it had to be vast. Earth is visited by a giant from Sirius, eight leagues tall, who joins forces with a lesser giant from Saturn, six fathoms tall. Voltaire used this scale to highlight the insignificance of humans and their ignorance in believing the heavens existed for their benefit.

The first star distances were calculated in the 1830s. Our closest star system is that of Alpha Centauri, 4.37 light years away, or over 25 million million miles. Thomas Henderson calculated the distance in 1833 but underestimated it. He withheld the data for six years fearing it would not be believed. The fastest form of transport at that time, the steam engine, travelled at 30 mph (50 kph), and would take almost 100 million years to reach the star.

How could anyone travel such distances? Voltaire, who was well acquainted with Newtonian physics, described Micromégas's travels as follows:

> Our voyager was very familiar with the laws of gravity and with all the other attractive and repulsive forces. He utilized them so well that, whether with the help of a ray of sunlight or some comet, he jumped from globe to globe like a bird vaulting itself from branch to branch.

The modern equivalent of jumping from globe to globe could be a form of 'gravity assist', or 'slingshot', which uses a planet's gravity to provide extra acceleration to a spacecraft. It was first proposed in fiction by Ray Cummings in his 1930 serial 'Brigands of the Moon'. It was not seriously considered in scientific circles until 1954 and was first used in 1974 when *Mariner 10* passed Venus on its way to Mercury.

Voltaire's reference to 'a ray of sunlight' could be interpreted today as the use of the solar wind, a phrase coined by the astrophysicist Eugene Parker in 1958.

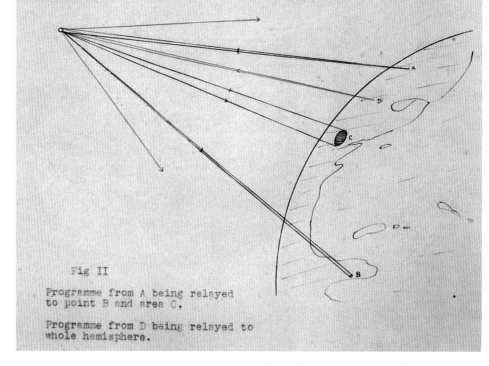

a reflector only a few feet across would give a beam so directive that almost all the power would be concentrated on the earth. Arrays a metre or so in diameter could be used to illuminate single countries if a more restricted service was required.

11.   The stations would be connected with each other by very-narrow-beam, low-power links, probably working in the optical spectrum or near it, so that beams less than a degree wide could be produced.

12.   The system would provide the following services which cannot be realised in any other manner:-

    a) Simultaneous television broadcasts to the entire globe, including services to aircraft.
    b) Relaying of programmes between distant parts of the planet.

13.   In addition the stations would make redundant the network of relay towers covering the main areas of civilisation and representing investments of hundreds of millions of pounds. (Work on the first of these networks has already started.)

14.   Figure II shows diagrammatically some of the specialised services that could be provided by the use of differing radiator systems.

Fig II

Programme from A being relayed to point B and area C.

Programme from D being relayed to whole hemisphere.

Above The original manuscript for Arthur C. Clarke's 1945 article 'The Space Station – It's Radio Applications' showing how a satellite in geo-stationary orbit can be used to relay radio and television across the globe.

Right Cover of *Analog*, April 1964, by Harvey Woolhiser showing a spaceship powered by the solar wind from 'Sunjammer' by Winston P. Sanders (a pen name of Poul Anderson).

Just imagine.
You are in a generation starship but don't realize that's what it is and no one remembers where it's going. What would life on that world be like?

Arthur C. Clarke (1917–2008)

British writer, long resident in Sri Lanka, known for *2001: A Space Odyssey* and for proposing a series of geostationary global communication satellites in 'Extra-Terrestrial Relays' (1945), seventeen years before the launch of *Telstar*. Clarke was passionate about rocketry and popularized space exploration through his books and his work with the British Interplanetary Society. An early essay was 'We Can Rocket to the Moon – Now!' (1938), and he believed science fiction would raise a greater awareness of space travel in 'Science Fiction: Preparation for the Space Age' (1953). Clarke's novels cover the full range of space exploration and colonization, from *Prelude to Space* (1951) about the first British expedition to the Moon to *The Songs of Distant Earth* (1986), where one of Earth's last spaceships reaches a remote human colony, and from *Islands in the Sky* (1952) about the earliest space stations (where a boy wins a trip on a TV game show) to *The City and the Stars* (1956) about the last domed city on Earth. Other major works, mostly positive about humanity and the cosmos, and often with a mystical sense of wonder, include *Childhood's End* (1953) where humans find they are being manipulated by a benign alien race, *Rendezvous with Rama* (1972) about a vast alien artefact that enters the solar system, and *The Fountains of Paradise* (1979) about the construction of a space elevator.

Jules Verne had wondered whether one day ships might be powered by light in *From the Earth to the Moon* (1865), but did not explore the idea. That charged particles from the Sun might 'power' a spaceship was first explored in detail by Carl Wiley in 1951 in 'Clipper Ships of Space' in *Astounding Science Fiction*. It was first used in science fiction by the enigmatic Cordwainer Smith in 'The Lady Who Sailed *The Soul*' (1960), but it was also used, perhaps surprisingly, by Pierre Boulle in *La Planète des singes* (*Planet of the Apes*, 1963).

In his novella 'Lumen' (in *Récits de l'infini*, 1872), Camille Flammarion recognized the physical limitation of the speed of light, but proposed that the soul survived the body and could travel in excess of lightspeed. However, in 1905 Albert Einstein published his special theory of relativity suggesting that the speed of light cannot be exceeded. Writers had to discover other means of travel. Fred T. Jane's idea in *To Venus in Five Seconds* (1897) was for a series of matter transmitters. Though the phrase was not used, this was the first 'beam me up' interplanetary story.

Amongst the early pulp writers, Edmond Hamilton and E.E. Smith opened up the cosmos in such extravaganzas as 'Crashing Suns' (1928) and *The Skylark of Space* (1928; book, 1946), but they ignored Einstein's theory. Their peer, John W. Campbell, Jr, later editor of *Astounding Science Fiction*, felt a need for more discipline. In *Islands of Space* (1931; book, 1956) he suggested that an energy field could warp space, creating a fold that acted as a short cut. He called the region within the fold 'hyperspace'. The idea has taken on new life with black holes and the concept of wormholes in space, created by collapsing stars, or collapsars as Joe Haldeman called them in *The Forever War* (1974). Arthur C. Clarke harnessed the power of a tiny black hole to generate power for an 'asymptotic drive', or a fusion-powered rocket, in *Imperial Earth* (1976).

The ramjet principle, first hinted at by Cyrano de Bergerac, was invented in 1913 by René Lorin. In 1960 Robert Bussard proposed a variant that used powerful electro-magnets to scoop hydrogen from the interstellar medium. In theory a spacecraft using this propulsion could reach speeds close to that of light. It has featured in several books by Larry Niven, notably *Protector* (1973), where it is called the ramscoop, and was a key feature of the novel *Tau Zero* (1970) by Poul Anderson, where a spaceship accelerates so fast that it passes from this universe to the next.

The alternative to faster-than-light travel is to send people to the stars either in suspended animation, as happened in Clarke's *2001: A Space Odyssey* (1968) and James White's *The Dream Millennium* (1974), or in a generation starship or interstellar ark, so that it is the descendants of the original crew who reach the destination. The space ark first appeared in fiction in 'The Voyage That Lasted 600 Years' (1940) by Don Wilcox. Other notable titles include 'Universe' (1941) by Robert A. Heinlein, incorporated into *Orphans of the Sky* (1963), *Non-Stop* (1958) by Brian W. Aldiss, Harry Martinson's epic poem *Aniara* (1956) and Gene Wolfe's equally epic four-volume sequence *The Book of the Long Sun* (1993–6). James Blish depicts whole cities taking to space in *Cities in Flight* (1970).

Science-fiction writers had adapted science in order to reach the stars, but the next big question was what would they find there.

"That's the one we headed for a thousand years ago."

by CLIFFORD D. SIMAK

Spacebred Generations

SCIENCE-FICTION +   AUGUST, 1953

Here at last is a different science-fiction story. Imagine a space ark launched from the Earth seeking another star system. The space ark is in transit for over 1,000 years, during which time the several thousand occupants are permanently imprisoned. What will be the sociological and other effects on these travelers? How will they live? What are the implications of time and isolation on their behavior, their lives, their thoughts, and their beliefs? Clifford D. Simak has painted a most daring yet logical picture of this situation. It is one of those rare stories that will start you thinking, and that you will remember.

THERE had been silence—for many generations. Then the silence ended.

The Mutter came at "dawn."

The Folk awoke, crouching in their beds, listening to the Mutter. It had been spoken that one day would come the Mutter? And that the Mutter would be the beginning of the End?

Jon Hoff awoke, and Mary Hoff, his wife.

They were the only two within their cubicle, for they had no children. They were not yet allowed a child. Before they could have a child the elderly Joshua must die before there would be room for it, and knowing this they had waited for his death, guilty at their unspoken prayer that he soon must die—willing him to die so they might have a child.

The Mutter came and ran throughout the Ship. Then the bed in which Jon and Mary crouched spun upward from the floor and crashed against the wall, pinning them against the humming metal, while all the other furniture—chest and chairs and table—came crashing from floor to wall, where it came to rest, as if the wall suddenly had become the floor and the floor the wall.

The Holy Picture dangled from the ceiling, which a moment before had been the other wall, hung there for a moment, swaying in the air; then it, too, crashed downward.

In that moment the Mutter ended and there was silence once again—but not the olden silence, for although there was no sound one could reach out and pinpoint, there were many sounds—a feeling, if not a hearing, of the sounds of surging power, of old machinery stirring back to life, of an old order, long dormant, taking over once again.

Jon Hoff crawled out part way from beneath the bed, then straightened on his arms, using his back to lift the bed so his wife could crawl out, too. Free of the bed, they stood on the wall-that-had-become-a-floor and saw the litter of the furniture, which had not been theirs alone, but had been used and then passed down to them through many generations.

For there was nothing wasted; there was nothing thrown away. That was the law—or one of many laws—that you could not waste, that you could not throw away. You used everything there was, down to the last shred of its utility. You ate only enough food—nor more, no less. You drank only enough water—no more, no less. You used the same air over and over again—literally the same air. The wastes of your body went into the converter to be changed into something that you, or someone else, would use again. Even the dead—you used the dead again. And there had been many dead in the long generations from the First Beginning. In months to come, some day perhaps not too

Although writing is but his avocation, Clifford D. Simak has had three books published, City, Cosmic Engineers, and Ring Around the Sun, supplemented by a dozen or more anthology inclusions.

4

5

Illustration by Tom O'Reilly depicting a generation starship from 'Spacebred Generations' by Clifford D. Simak, *Science Fiction Plus*, August 1953.

September • 50 cents

analog

SCIENCE FACT ⌒ SCIENCE FICTION

A LIFE FOR THE STARS by Jam

A story of the industrial cities of sp

PDC

Space Travel

JULY 1958 · 35¢

TODAY'S CHALLENGE:
SATELLITES TO A
SPACE STATION

Cover of *Analog*, September 1962,
by George Solonevich, depicting
one of the cities in flight powered
by James Blish's spindizzy in 'A Life for
the Stars'.

Malcolm Smith's portrayal of
a space station orbiting Earth
on the cover of *Space Travel*,
July 1958.

The earliest writers usually portrayed intelligent extraterrestrials as humanoid and little thought was given to how they might have evolved according to their alien environment. The very idea that creatures could evolve was contrary to both church belief and, until at least the late eighteenth century, most scientific thinking. Writers had fun depicting life on the Moon, much like Mandeville and Swift had on Earth – Lucian had his dog-faced men and flea archers, Cyrano his horse-men and intelligent birds – but none of these was developed on a scientific basis. Only Johannes Kepler tried to relate his lunar inhabitants to their environment in *Somnium* (1634) by recognizing their need to adapt to the extremes of temperature during the long days and nights.

It was with the publication of Charles Darwin's *On the Origin of Species* (1859), alongside the growth of palaeontology, particularly the work on dinosaur fossils by Richard Owen in the 1860s, that the evolution and diversity of life on Earth was highlighted. How more diverse might it be throughout the cosmos?

The first truly non-human aliens arrive from another dimension rather than space, in 'Les Xipéhuz' (1887) by the Belgian-French writer Joseph-Henri Boëx, writing as J.H. Rosny. They appear in ancient Mesopotamia about 5000 BC and take various shapes – cylindrical, conical, flat, crystalline – depending on their stage of development. They are ruthless and it requires considerable cunning and bravery amongst the local tribesmen to overcome them.

It was H.G. Wells who popularized the idea of hostile 'aliens' with his invading Martians in *The War of the Worlds* (1898). The modern-day descendants of Wells's Martians, intellectually advanced but with feeble bodies encased in machines, are the Daleks, created by Terry Nation and first featured in *Dr Who* in December 1963. The idea that aliens are best depicted as soulless machines or cyborgs has proved appealing. *Dr Who*

repeated the success in 1966 with the Cybermen. Their equivalent in the *Star Trek* universe are the Borg, created by Maurice Hurley. These cybernetically-enhanced humanoid drones that function within a collective hive-mind first appeared in the episode 'Q Who?' in May 1989.

Similar are the machine intelligences the Berserkers, created by Fred Saberhagen – the early stories collected in *Berserker* (1967). These are doomsday machines left over from an ancient interplanetary war that have continued to seek out and destroy sentient life. In *Across the Sea of Suns* (1984), part of his Galactic Center

Saga, Gregory Benford introduced the Mechs, another form of self-replicating machine intent on destroying organic life.

As far back as 1872 Samuel Butler had suggested in *Erewhon* that machines would evolve faster than humans to the point that humans would become subservient to them. The Hungarian author Frigyes Karinthy used this idea in his sequel to *Gulliver's Travels*, *Utazás Faremidóba* (*Voyage to Faremido*, 1916), where Gulliver is taken to the planet Faremido and encounters benign intelligent machines that communicate by musical sounds.

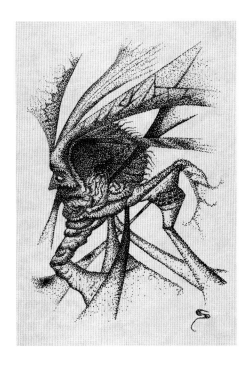

Left Sir Arthur Conan Doyle conjectured that alien beings might already exist on Earth. In 'The Horror of the Heights' (1913) an aviator ventures into the upper atmosphere and discovers floating jellyfish and vicious predators, here illustrated by W.R.S. Stott in *The Strand Magazine*, November 1913.
P.P.6004.glk

Above Illustration of an alien creature from *Jenseits-Galerie* (1907) by Paul Scheerbart. This was a portfolio of aliens which Scheerbart described as representing 'what we have seen beyond the Orbit of Neptune'.
X.423/2606

The astronomer Camille Flammarion held a life-long interest in extraterrestrial life, which he first considered in *La Pluralité des mondes habités* (*The Plurality of Inhabited Worlds*, 1862). In *Uranie* (1890) the narrator travels throughout the cosmos and encounters a huge variety of life, from beings that pupate and are reborn, to luminous creatures or dragonfly-like intelligences that live in symbiosis with plants. He was simply translating the diversity of life on Earth to the stars and emphasized how alien life need not be humanoid. Olaf Stapledon did the same in *Star Maker* (1937), which explores the history of the universe, chronicling the cycles of existence of many diverse life forms. This includes sentient stars and, ultimately, the Star Maker itself, the being that created the universe.

Science fiction writers in the pulp magazines delighted in horrible alien creatures. In his Interstellar Patrol series, serialized in *Weird Tales* in 1929 (book, *Crashing Suns*, 1965), Edmond Hamilton featured a different bizarre alien for each story – cone-shaped, amoeboid, cuboid, gaseous – but none had any evolutionary basis. It was diversity for its own sake. It was in the 1930s pulps that the stereotypical bug-eyed monsters emerged, such as those from Andromeda in 'The Conquest of Earth' (1930) by Isaac R. Nathanson. Unfortunately this desire for monstrous and often ridiculous aliens flourished in post-war/Cold War B-movies, such as *Godzilla* (1954) and *The Blob* (1958), which did much to ruin the reputation of science fiction and establish the stereotypical image of all that is bad about 'sci fi'. Films like *Alien* (1979) and *E.T.* (1982) have to some degree helped rectify that image.

Other pulp writers did attempt to create believable aliens in their own world. In 'A Martian Odyssey' (1934) by Stanley G. Weinbaum, a stranded astronaut saves a birdlike creature, Tweel, and the two travel together, encountering many strange beings. Weinbaum created an ecology that existed by its own rules, without necessarily making sense to humans.

Creating a truly alien world, with its flora and fauna, requires specialist knowledge. One of the first was Hal Clement, the writing alias of science teacher Harry Stubbs. His planet Mesklin, depicted in *Mission of Gravity* (1954) and various sequels, is a giant oblated sphere, four times the diameter of the Earth at the equator but only twice at the poles. That is because it revolves very fast, with a day only nine minutes long. The centrifugal force almost cancels out the extreme gravity, with three times Earth's gravity at the equator but over 600G at the poles. The seas are liquid methane, the atmosphere ammonia. Humans can barely survive there, but when a research probe malfunctions at the South Pole they need to find it and seek the help of a native Mesklinite, who is 45cm long and looks like a centipede.

Clement's achievement inspired others. Harry Harrison created the hostile world of Pyrrus in *Deathworld* (1960), which has been colonized because of its extensive ores. It is a high-gravity, radioactive world with severe weather, huge tidal changes, frequent earthquakes and volcanic activity, and all native animals and plants are hostile or poisonous.

Perhaps the most extreme inhabited environment is that described in *Dragon's Egg* (1980) by Robert L. Forward. Living on a neutron star with gravitation 67 billion times that of Earth are the cheela, intelligent beings the size of sesame seeds, whose lifetime is a matter of minutes and whose civilization evolves in months.

In *The Black Cloud* (1957) by Fred Hoyle, humanity is endangered by a giant organic cloud in space that is unaware of any intelligent life on Earth. In Stanisław Lem's *Solaris* (1961), scientists discover that the ocean covering the eponymous planet is one vast sentient organism, which is studying them. When Isaac Asimov returned to the Foundation series with *Foundation's Edge*

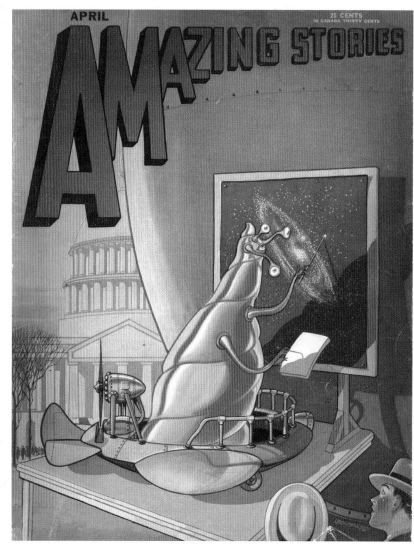

Top left Cover of the August 1970 *Analog*, by Kelly Freas, depicting the inhospitable planet Mesklin in Hal Clement's sequel to *Mission of Gravity, Star Light.*
P.P.6383.agk

Above 'The Conquest of the Earth' by Isaac R. Nathanson, *Amazing Stories*, April 1930, illustrated by Leo Morey.
P.P.6383.ccs

Left Back cover of *Fantastic Adventures*, September 1939 showing 'Life on Mercury' by Frank R. Paul, suggesting that any life there could only be in insect form.

Right *Deathworld* by Harry Harrison, *Astounding*, January 1960, illustrated by Henry van Dongen.

Far right 'The Big Trek' by Fritz Leiber, *The Magazine of Fantasy and Science Fiction*, October 1957, illustrated by Ed Emshwiller's. A man finds himself amidst a host of alien visitors who have come to a devastated Earth one last time to see the ruins.

Astounding
SCIENCE FICTION

Jan. 1960 · 50 Cents

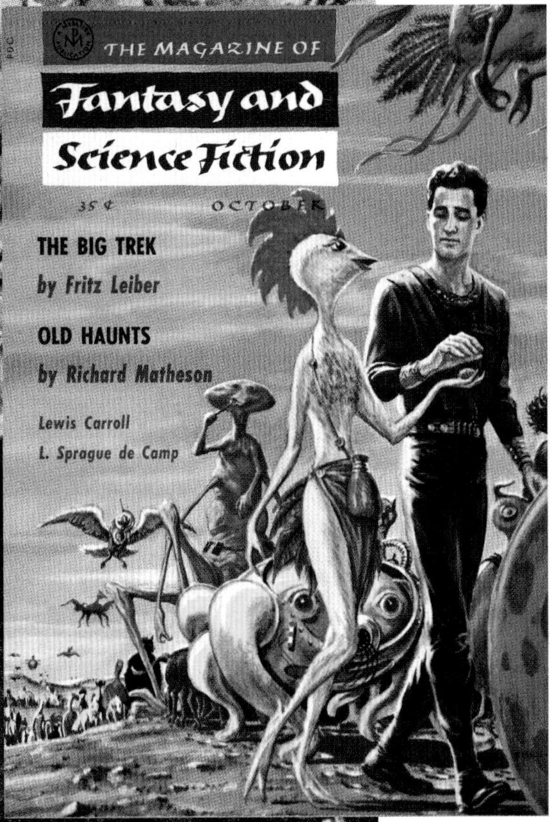

THE MAGAZINE OF

Fantasy and Science Fiction

35¢   OCTOBER

THE BIG TREK
by Fritz Leiber

OLD HAUNTS
by Richard Matheson

Lewis Carroll
L. Sprague de Camp

DEATHWORLD, By Harry Harrison

(1982) he revealed the marvels of the planet Gaia where every living creature is linked telepathically as one consciousness that extends to inorganic material, thus making it a living planet.

In his Sector General series, James White describes a hospital in space that treats every kind of alien, up to planet size, and is staffed by a variety of extraterrestrials, all of whom regard themselves as 'human' but see the human beings as 'alien'.

In *Ring* (1994), the fourth novel of his Xeelee sequence, Stephen Baxter introduced the photino birds, creatures of dark matter that drain stars of energy to prematurely age them. The Caleban in Frank Herbert's *Whipping Star* (1970) exist across all dimensions and have such huge power that they appear to humans as stars.

Of course, planetary environments and life forms do not have to be extreme. Planets suited to colonization should ideally be Earth-like with compliant natives where contact can easily be made. This raises the matter of communication. If we cannot communicate with even the most intelligent animals on Earth, how can we hope to do so with alien species? For that matter, how do you know the degree of intelligence of any alien life form you encounter? A. Bertram Chandler tackled this in 'The Cage' (1957). A party of humans exploring an alien world are captured by other alien explorers and exhibited in a cage. The humans cannot convince the aliens of their intelligence until they capture a small creature and put it into a cage. That convinces the aliens, because only sentient beings place other creatures in cages.

The most convenient form of non-verbal communication is telepathy, which has been used since at least *Lieut. Gullivar Jones, His Vacation* (1905) by Edwin Lester Arnold. Other methods may be by music, made famous in the film *Close Encounters of the Third Kind* (1977) but used as far back as Cyrano's Moon voyage; by dance, as in 'The Dance of the Changer and Three' (1968) by Terry Carr; by colour, in *VOR* (1958) by James Blish; by mathematics, in *Neverness* (1988) by David Zindell; or by gesture, in 'The Gift of Gab' (1955) by Jack Vance. Vance is one of several writers – C.J. Cherryh, Samuel Delany and Ian Watson being

James White (1928–99)

Ulster-born writer, best known for his Sector General series set on a space station/hospital staffed by 10,000 extraterrestrials. The first stories appeared in *New Worlds* magazine and were collected as *Hospital Station* (1962), followed by a novel, *Star Surgeon* (1963). White periodically returned to the series, which ran to twelve books by the time of his death with *Double Contact* (1999). The series' appeal is partly because of the problems facing the staff due to the variety of creatures they have to treat, with the related personal and moral issues that arise, and partly by White's emphasis on the co-operation between different species. White was a pacifist, and living in Northern Ireland during the Troubles gave greater emphasis to his desire for peace and harmony. White's views came to the boil in the uncharacteristic *Underkill* (1979), a freestanding novel where an alien race, tired of the savagery of humans, decides that the species needs to be eradicated.

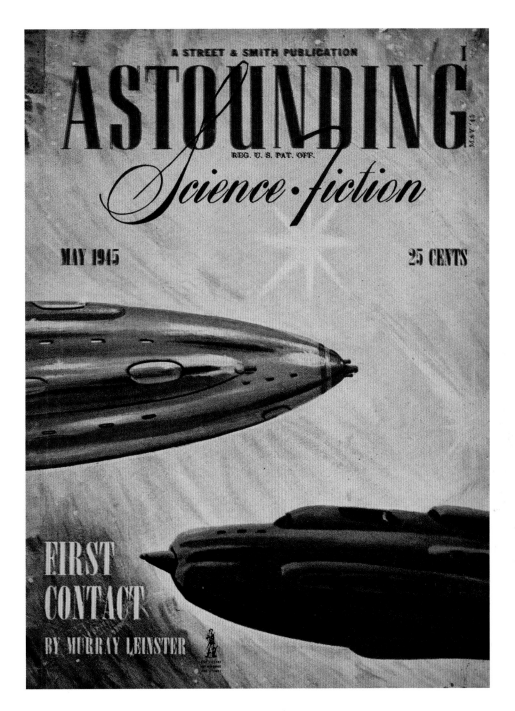

others – who have explored languages and their impact in a number of their books, notably Delany's *Babel-17* (1966) and Cherryh's *Hunter of Worlds* (1977).

One of the most profound books on understanding and communicating with alien life is *Memoirs of a Spacewoman* (1962) by Naomi Mitchison, a highly personal account of both the woman astronaut charged with studying alien life and the cultures she observes. At times she finds it difficult to remain objective, which leads to breaking the code of non-interference. This convention, now known as the Prime Directive since being enshrined in Starfleet regulations in *Star Trek*, states that there should be no interference with the development of another planet's culture. It seems to have first been used by Olaf Stapledon in *Star Maker*.

Communication is crucial to how humans will understand and relate to extraterrestrials. Amongst many such stories, one of the first to tackle it head-on was 'First Contact' (1945) by Murray Leinster, which considered what would happen when a human and an alien spacecraft meet in space. How do you know how the other side will react, and what do you do to ensure each other's safety? Leinster believed that you start from a position of distrust and work towards a common understanding. Ivan Yefremov reversed the thinking in 'Cor Serpentis' ('The Heart of the Serpent', 1958), taking the view that a culture that is sufficiently advanced to have space exploration must have already established a harmonic equilibrium at home and therefore any intelligence encountered in space would be peaceful. How certain can that be?

Just imagine. Exploring an alien world you encounter a large non-human creature. It remains still. What would you do and how could you determine the creature's intelligence?

Following exploration will come colonization, and the first step to the stars will be the Moon and Mars. It was realized quite early that at some stage the Moon would seek independence from Earth, as told in 'The Birth of a New Republic' (1931) by Miles J. Breuer and Jack Williamson and again in *The Moon is a Harsh Mistress* (1966) by Robert A. Heinlein, both of which developed parallels with the American War of Independence. In similar vein, *Steel Beach* (1992) by John Varley, and *Moonrise* (1996) and *Moonwar* (1998) by Ben Bova, look at how lunar colonists struggle to maintain their existence.

The first truly iconic book about the colonization of Mars was *The Martian Chronicles* (1950) by Ray Bradbury. Drawn together from stories written during the 1940s, the book follows the families who settle on Mars and their early conflict with the native Martians who die out because of human viruses. A nuclear war on Earth removes the chance of returning home, and the settlers realize that they are now the Martians.

For Mars to be a viable colony it would need to be adapted to Earth-like conditions, a process called terraforming. The word was coined by Jack Williamson in the story 'Collision Orbit' (1942), though there he applied it to an asteroid. The most extensive set of books about terraforming Mars is the trilogy *Red Mars* (1992), *Green Mars* (1993) and *Blue Mars* (1996) by Kim Stanley Robinson. Few other planets within the solar system are suitable for terraforming, though Pamela Sargent gave Venus the treatment in her ambitious trilogy, *Venus of Dreams* (1986), *Venus of Shadows* (1988) and *Child of Venus* (2001).

Beyond the solar system writers could work from a blank sheet and create their own worlds and cultures. The earliest to consider an extended planetary civilization, and a non-human one at that, was French physician C.I. Defontenay with *Star ou Psi de Cassiopée* (1854). Forgotten, even in France, for almost a century and not translated into

English until 1975, as *Star (Psi Cassiopeia)*, the book describes the conflicting societies on a planet within a complex system around the star Psi Cassiopeia.

Once humanity has spread to the stars individual colonies may expand into an empire. Robert W. Cole foresaw this in *The Struggle for Empire* (1900) with conflict between the Anglo-Saxon Empire, which controls the solar system, and the Sirian Empire over planetary borders. Cole's novel parallels the power alliances in Europe prior to the First World War.

The popularity of galactic empires owes much to the Foundation series by Isaac Asimov, which began in *Astounding Science Fiction* in 1942 and was collected in three volumes, starting with *Foundation* (1951), to which several more have since been added. Asimov envisaged a galactic empire, modelled on the Roman Empire, developing thousands of years in the future. Its capital becomes the planet Trantor close to the galactic hub. The main

Above left *The Martian Chronicles* by Ray Bradbury. This was the second edition in 1958 with a new dust jacket by Robert Watson that Bradbury preferred.

Above *Asimov's Science Fiction*, February 1994. Cover by Todd Lockwood for 'Martian Childhood' by Kim Stanley Robinson.

story deals with a mathematician who has predicted the fall of the empire and an extensive dark age before the rise of a new empire. To minimize the damage he establishes two remote foundations as storehouses of all human knowledge.

Asimov established a template that has been used by many and was popularized in the *Star Wars* films. In the bestselling series that began with *Dune* (1965), Frank Herbert depicted a huge interstellar empire, twenty thousand years in the future, feudal in nature, reminiscent of the Holy Roman Empire in the Middle Ages. There is conflict between the ruling houses with the focus on the planet Arrakis, the sole source of the spice *melange* which has become the most valuable substance in the universe. Arrakis is a hostile sand planet, inhabited by the native Fremen who alone control the giant sandworms and who believe that one day they will have a saviour who will transform their world.

Similar galactic empires with rivalry between ruling factions appear in *Nova* (1968) by Samuel R. Delany and the Saga of the Skolian Empire series by Catherine Asaro, starting with *Primary Inversion* (1995). Only a few authors have considered the overall history of the Empire. One notable exception is Poul Anderson, whose novels of the Psychotechnic League follow humanity's expansion into space, succeeded by the Polesotechnic League of interstellar traders that grew into the Terran Empire. This is covered in over thirty books from *The Snows of Ganymede* (1955; book, 1958) to *The Game of Empire* (1985).

A variant on the theme was created by Iain M. Banks in his Culture series, starting with *Consider Phlebas* (1987). The Culture is an interstellar multi-species society of over 30 trillion citizens that live not only on planets but also in world ships and ringworlds controlled by artificial intelligences. When Earth was first contacted, the Culture had been in existence for millennia. This approach has appealed to British writers, and similar networks feature in the works of Stephen

Above John Schoenherr's iconic cover for *Analog*, March 1965, depicting the giant sandworm from Frank Herbert's serial, 'The Prophet of Dune'.

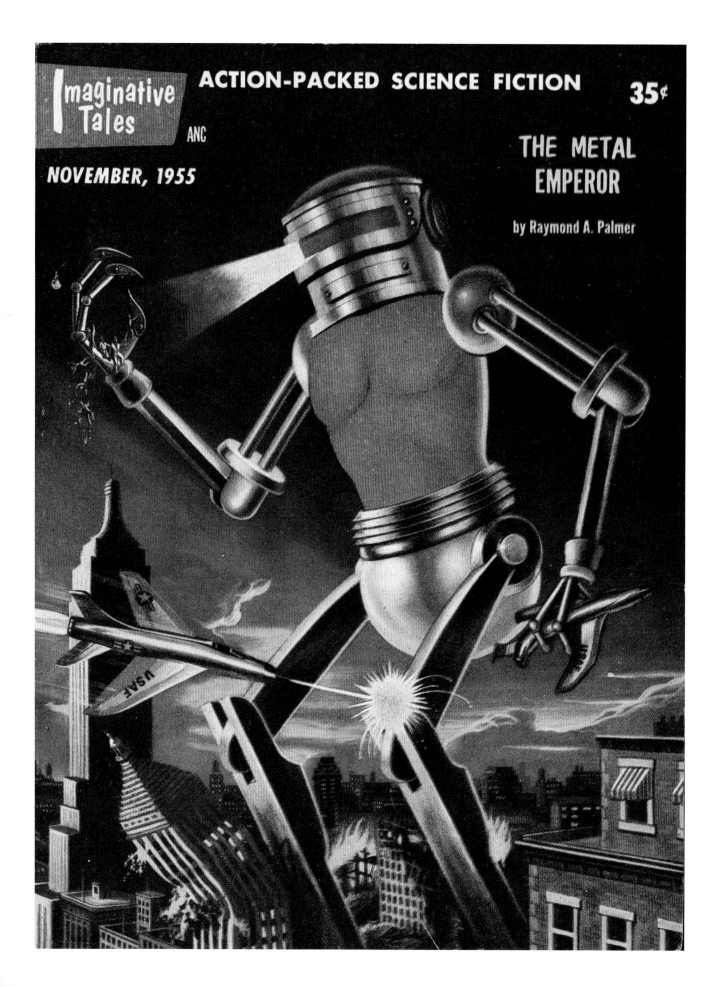

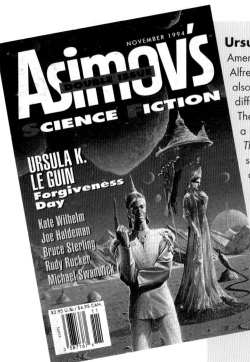

Ursula K. Le Guin (born 1929)

American multi-award winning writer of science fiction and fantasy, daughter of anthropologists Alfred and Theodora Kroeber. Renowned for her Earthsea series of fantasies, Le Guin has also produced a series of novels and stories generally known as the Hainish Cycle, exploring different aspects of a League of All Worlds (or Ekumen) at different periods of its development. The novels, starting with *Rocannon's World* (1966), are not sequential but do establish a broad tapestry. They include two of the most notable works of modern science fiction, *The Left Hand of Darkness* (1969) and *The Dispossessed* (1974). The background to the series is that long ago the humanoid Hain colonized many worlds. Those on some planets developed naturally, others were genetically manipulated, leading to significant diversity before the Hain civilization collapsed. Millennia pass and the Ekumen are seeking to rediscover these worlds and establish a League. *The Left Hand of Darkness* takes place on the planet Gethen, where the inhabitants are of one gender and where, perhaps as a consequence, there has never been any warfare. Through the perspective of a visiting envoy, Le Guin observes how an androgynous culture might function. *The Dispossessed*, the earliest of the novels in internal sequence, explores the relationship between a planet, which retains capitalist values, and its moon, which has been colonized by revolutionaries to create an anarchy. Neither is the utopia they desire, although together they could form a whole. Both novels explore unity and division.

Asimov's Science Fiction, November 1994. Cover by Terry Czeczko for 'Forgiveness Day' by Ursula K. Le Guin. This story, incorporated into her book *Four Ways to Forgiveness* (1995) is part of her Ekumen series.

Left Painting by Lloyd Rognan for the cover of *Imaginative Tales*, November 1955 around which Raymond A. Palmer wrote his novella of an alien menace, 'The Metal Emperor'.

Right *Galaxy*, August 1962, featuring 'The Dragon Masters' by Jack Vance, illustrated by Jack Gaughan. Despite the title this is science fiction, one of Vance's many set amongst distant human colonies on alien worlds.

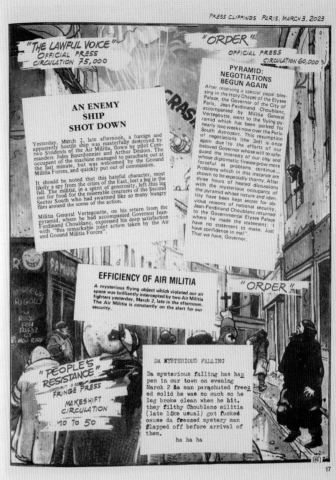

Baxter, Alastair Reynolds and Peter F. Hamilton. Likewise, David Brin's Uplift series of novels, starting with *Sundiver* (1980), envisages an ever-expanding galactic civilization that assists the emergence of new sentient species.

Other writers have recognized the galactic template but have focused on specific planets or groups of planets, where humans have either established themselves in harmony with the indigenous fauna or are still striving to overcome major obstacles.

One such is the Pern series by Anne McCaffrey, which began with *Dragonflight* (1968) and has extended to almost twenty books, covering the colonization of Pern and its development as an agrarian culture. Humans have learned to live in symbiosis with the native fire-lizards, which have been genetically enhanced as the eponymous 'dragons', and which protect the colony from the destructive 'thread'.

In her Canopus in Argos series of five novels, Doris Lessing draws upon science fiction, religion and fable to build a variety of societies where she can explore a range of philosophical and sociological issues. Her template is that there are vastly superior planetary civilizations, most notably the Canopeans, who have helped develop and steer life on various planets via accelerated evolution. This includes Earth, known to them as Shikasta in the opening book, *Re: Colonised Planet 5, Shikasta* (1979). The sequence, particularly *The Sirian Experiments* (1980), considers the implications of colonialism, such as that experienced in the British Empire, and how aspirations and hopes may be helped or hindered by competing overlords.

Brian Aldiss also explored the implications of colonial interference in his Helliconia trilogy, which began with *Helliconia Spring* (1982). Helliconia is the only planet humans have discovered to sustain advanced life, including a humanoid race. Rather than interfere with the planet, humans have been monitoring it from an orbiting space station for centuries, through several degenerating generations. Helliconia is recovering from a 1000-year long winter and civilization is trying to re-establish itself.

The idea of exploring planetary societies over long series has appealed ever since Edgar Rice Burroughs developed his Martian series with 'Under the Moons of Mars' (1912; book, as *A Princess of Mars*, 1917). Burroughs's stories became known as planetary romances ('romance' in its original meaning of 'adventure') and these became increasingly popular from the 1940s to the 1970s. Writers who fell under Burroughs' spell and produced similar work include Leigh Brackett, Marion Zimmer Bradley, Michael Moorcock and Jack Vance.

Jack Vance may well have created more human-alien societies than any other writer. He developed the planetary romance on a galactic scale in such books

中国科幻基石丛书
中国科幻银河奖特别奖获奖作品　　刘慈欣 著

三体
"地球往事" 三部曲之一
重庆出版集团 重庆出版社

as *Big Planet* (1957), *The Languages of Pao* (1958) and *The Star King* (1964). Most of Vance's books fall into one of several series, including the Alastor and Durdane trilogies, all notable for the creation of exotic, often picaresque or feudal worlds, detailing power struggles within a loosely connected empire. In similar vein is Robert Silverberg's series set on the huge multi-species planet Majipoor, which began with *Lord Valentine's Castle* (1980).

Earth's history of colonialism is notorious for its effect upon native cultures, and it could be repeated in space. In *Skylark Three* (1930; book, 1948), E.E. Smith destroyed the home planet of the Fenachrone because they regarded themselves as the lords of the universe. There was a shift against this in stories such as Edmond Hamilton's 'A Conquest of Two Worlds' (1932) and P. Schuyler Miller's 'The Forgotten Man of Space' (1933), where individuals stood against the destruction of native species. But the show of military might has continued in science fiction, depicting interstellar wars between humans and other races, as in Robert A. Heinlein's *Starship Troopers* (1959) and Joe Haldeman's *The Forever War* (1974).

The reverse could also happen. The threat of an alien invasion has remained vivid since H.G. Wells's *The War of the Worlds* (1898) and seems all the more dominant if the aliens are conquering Earth as part of their own colonial expansion. Octavia E. Butler provided a powerful example in her Xenogenesis trilogy (also called Lilith's Brood): *Dawn*, *Adulthood Rites* and *Imago* (1987–9). Humanity has all but destroyed itself in a nuclear war and the survivors have been 'rescued' by the Oankali who

seek out alien species in order to breed and thus diversify their genetically mutated and defective genes. The price for being rescued, particularly for the human women, is to become mating stock. Butler powerfully relates this form of 'benign' overlordship to that imposed upon slaves in the Americas.

The popular Chinese author Liu Cixin has developed another angle in his San Ti (Three Bodies) trilogy, which began with *San Ti* (2007). In the first novel

China makes contact with an alien race, but receives a warning that this race is bloodthirsty and warlike. Once alerted to Earth the aliens prepare to invade, but their journey will take 400 years, giving Earth time to prepare sufficiently advanced technology to combat the menace.

These books forewarn us that when we do set forth to colonize the stars we should learn from history, and we must be prepared for those who might seek to colonize us.

Time and Parallel Worlds

What is time?

In his 1919 short story 'The Girl in the Golden Atom', Ray Cummings wittily wrote, 'Time is what stops everything happening at once.' Time is duration – it is how we perceive the past, the present and the future. One concept of time is that it is linear, with all events happening in sequence, though our perception is always of the present.

But what is the present? How long does it last? That last sentence you read is now in the past. And that one. The present, therefore, lasts for an instant. Once that moment has gone it is in the past never to be recovered, and is replaced by moments from the future. Time thus appears to be a stream, flowing from the future into the past. Yet if that is so, where does it come from? What is the future?

To counter the linear time concept, Immanuel Kant, in his *Critique of Pure Reason* (1781), suggested that time is a psychological construct created by the mind so as to impose order upon events. Time does not exist of itself but is the way we perceive events.

However, the psychological perception of time raises other questions. How often have we said 'time flies' or 'doesn't time drag'? This tells us that the way we perceive the passage of time is different to the steady measure of the clock.

In *An Experiment with Time* (1927), J.W. Dunne proposed that all time exists at once and that although our conscious mind can only see the present our subconscious mind can see both past and future, which may manifest in our dreams.

Albert Einstein, in his special theory of relativity, showed that time and space are connected and that time may be measured differently by two different observers depending upon their relative velocities. This suggests that there is not only a psychological perception of time, but also a physical difference dependent upon time and motion.

The mystery of time provides ample material for writers. The best known idea is that of time travel. But what are the consequences? Time travel raises many paradoxes, such as what happens if you go back and kill your grandfather before your parents are conceived? Or you warn yourself to take a different course of action? How do you know that has not already happened? There would be trillions of alternate worlds created every moment.

Is it possible to shift sideways in time to an alternate world? One where, for example, Adolf Hitler had been victorious in World War II, or Abraham Lincoln had not been assassinated. What of those more personal events such as you had never met your partner? How might your life have changed?

Writers have explored many of these infinite worlds of proability: alternate worlds, parallel worlds, time slowed down or accelerated, the consequences of journeys into the past or the future, and other dimensions. That is what this section covers.

Right David A. Hardy's painting, *Portals to Infinity.*

Concepts of Time

The idea that time may not be the same everywhere is not new. In folklore, the world of 'faery' is often said to exist on a different timescale. In Ludwig Tieck's 'Die Elfen' ('The Elves', 1811) a young girl plays with the elves in a wood; when she goes back home she discovers many years have passed. The eighth-century Japanese story of Urashima Taro tells of a fisherman who enters an undersea world and lives with a princess for three years; when he returns, three centuries have gone by.

Washington Irving picked up the idea in 'The Adelantado of the Seven Cities' (1839). Here, a cavalier finds a fabled lost island, but on returning home he learns that time has moved on by a century. This concept recurs in many fantasies, most memorably in the Narnia books by C.S. Lewis. In *The Lion, the Witch and the Wardrobe* (1950) the reverse happens – the children spend many weeks in Narnia, but return home the same afternoon that they left.

The authors give no reason for the time differential, yet it bears comparison with one aspect of Einstein's theory of special relativity, propounded in 1905. He stated that time will pass differently for individuals who are moving at extremely high velocities relative to others who are not. So if a spaceship is able to reach close to lightspeed, time will appear to move slower onboard relative to those back on Earth. Anyone travelling to the stars will find when they return to Earth, centuries have passed. This is called time dilation.

The idea of using time dilation to travel into the future was not picked up immediately by science-fiction writers, and Nebraskan doctor Miles J. Breuer may have been the first. In 'The Fitzgerald Contraction' and 'The Time Valve' (both 1930) Lunarians – in the distant past (when the Moon was inhabited) – test a starship, but on their return find the Moon is long dead. They visit Earth and humans take the starship to explore the future. Time dilation is central to *No World of Their Own* (1955) by Poul Anderson, *The Forever War* (1974) by Joe Haldeman,

A World Out of Time (1976) by Larry Niven and *The Sparrow* (1996) by Mary Doria Russell, whilst 'Common Time' (1953) by James Blish considers subjective time for the first interstellar astronaut.

Thirty years before Einstein, the French astronomer Camille Flammarion had his own views on relativity. In 'Lumen' (in *Récits de l'infini*, 1872), he proposed that if you exceed the velocity of light you would see the Earth in the past by 'historic light'. The French-born Jean Delaire developed the idea in *Around a Distant Star* (1904), where a Tesla-inspired scientist travels to a planet almost 2000 light-years away and, focusing a super-telescope on Earth, witnesses the crucifixion of Christ. The idea of 'historic light' intrigued Maurice Renard, though it was years before he completed *Le Maître de la lumière* (*The Master of Light*, 1933; book, 1947). His scientist creates 'luminite', a glass that slows down the passage of light and provides a window on the past. The same idea was developed independently by Bob Shaw as 'slow glass', in a series of stories novelized as *Other Days, Other Eyes* (1972).

Flammarion's 'historic light' also intrigued the French humorist Eugène Mouton who created a time viewer, in the form of a super-telescope, in 'L'historioscope' (in *Fantaisies*, 1883). A time viewer is a convenient way of watching the past without interacting with it. In *The Vicarion* (1926), Gardner Hunting uses one to help solve a crime. John Taine's viewer in *Before the Dawn* (1934) is powerful enough to observe the passing of the dinosaurs. However, starting with 'E for Effort' (1947) by T.L. Sherred, authors realized that a time viewer would be a universal Peeping Tom and that there would be no more secrets, a concept explored in Isaac Asimov's 'The Dead Past' (1956), Damon Knight's 'I See You' (1976) and *The Light of Other Days* (2000) by Arthur C. Clarke and Stephen Baxter.

Camille Flammarion also suggested that if you leave the Earth at greater than lightspeed you would see events on Earth

in reverse, and he describes in detail the dead coming alive during the battle of Waterloo. Suitably inspired, Albert Robida used the idea for a novel in *L'Horloge des siècles* (*The Clock of the Centuries*, 1902). Here the world is disrupted by catastrophes that prove to be the universe readjusting before moving in reverse. Everything happens backwards though still appears to individuals as happening in sequence. Other stories that have considered individuals living in reverse include 'The Curious Case of Benjamin Button' (1922) by F. Scott Fitzgerald and *Time's Arrow* (1991) by Martin Amis, whilst *Counter-Clock World* (1967) by Philip K. Dick and *An Age* (1967; in US as *Cryptozoic!*) by Brian W. Aldiss explore wider consequences. In Dicks' novel time is literally reversed. as in Flammarion's book. In Aldiss's novel, however, in which mental time travel is achieved through a new drug, human consciousness shifts into reverse, revealing the true nature of time.

All the above assume that time is a continuum. J.W. Dunne, however, believed that all time exists simultaneously. The conscious mind can only perceive the present, but in our dreams our consciousness is unshackled and is aware of all time. Starting in 1898, Dunne recorded his dreams and identified many as precognitive. He evaluated his theory in the highly influential *An Experiment with Time* (1927) and *The Serial Universe* (1934). These works not only gave an explanation for precognition, but also debated freewill versus predestination and provided a basis for psychic time travel. Stories adapting Dunne's views are often of a metaphysical nature, such as Algernon Blackwood's 'The Man Who Lived Backwards' (1930), where a man has a vision of his whole existence, or John Buchan's *The Gap in the Curtain*

Right Miles J. Breuer's 'The Time Valve', *Wonder Stories*, July 1930, illustrated by Frank R. Paul.
P.903/133

(228)

between one rain-fall and the next. ~~To expect anything to
flower here except for a few~~ tenacious ~~cacti of the
spirit xxxxxxxxxxxxxx was to shut one's eyes to reality.~~

~~Like a man in a deserted city where all the~~ other clocks
~~have stopped, he~~ was still obsessively ~~xxxxxxxxxxx~~ his
wrist-watch. He remembered the painting by Tanguy that he
had once treasured. Its drained beaches, eroded ~~xxx~~ of all
associations, of all sense of time, ~~was a~~ photographic
portrait of the salt world of the shore.

Ransom looked down at Judith as gazed distractedly at
the stove, ~~brushed his hair with an ~~ Despite
the ~~five~~ years together, the five arctic winters and ~~xxxxx~~
fierce summers when the salt banks gleamed like causeways
of chalk, ~~xxxxx despite the bonds of obligation and
dependence, and everything else he owed her~~, he felt
~~little sense of loyalty towards her.~~ The success if such
~~a term could be used~~ of their present ~~xxxxx~~ union, like
its failure ~~before they~~ ~~came to the coast~~ had been
decided by ~~completely~~ impersonal considerations.

"I'll bring one of the fish down, ~~he said, getting to
his feet.~~ "We'll have one meat for."

"~~Do you think we~~ can spare it?"

"Why not? ~~You never know,~~ perhaps there'll be a
tidal wave tonight."

J.G. Ballard (1930–2009)

English novelist and short story writer, closely associated with the New Wave movement in science fiction in the 1960s, but also renowned for his autobiographical novel *Empire of the Sun* (1984) and his urban novels *Crash* (1973), *Concrete Island* (1974) and *High-Rise* (1975). Ballard's short stories first appeared in *New Worlds* and *Science Fantasy* in 1956 and readers soon recognized their distinctive attitude and content, unlike anything else in the more traditional science-fiction magazines. Ballard's perceptions of reality had clearly been influenced by his two-and-a-half years in a Japanese internment camp in Shanghai during World War II. All of his stories challenge our perceptions and question our understanding of the world by re-interpreting the landscape. In Ballard's eyes the world is running down, entropy is maximizing and time has become a paralyzing stasis. In his key stories 'The Voices of Time' (1960) and 'The Terminal Beach' (1964), we find time degrading, creating a psychologically distorting environment. This pattern repeats in 'Myths of the Near Future' (1982), 'News from the Sun' (1981) and 'Memories of the Space Age' (1982), where individuals try to escape this timeless world through an inner transcendence.

J.G. Ballard, photograph by Fay Godwin, 1984.

Left A page from an early draft (entitled 'The Illuminated River') of chapter 27 of J.G. Ballard's *The Burning World* (1964; UK as *The Drought*, 1965). His manual revisions, in the top-left corner, describe a beach where 'time was not absent but immobilised'. Ballard's characterisation of the beach as a zone trapped in time calls to mind his contemporaneous story, 'The Terminal Beach' (1964).

Right Special J.G. Ballard issue of *Interzone*, April 1996, cover by SMS.

P.903/835

APRIL 1996

interZone 106

£2.75

J.G. Ballard

Special issue with his new story 'The Dying Fall'

plus stories by

Richard Calder

Terry Dowling

Ian Watson

HUGO AWARD WINNER

Scene from George Roy Hill's 1972
film adaptation of Kurt Vonnegut's
Slaughterhouse-Five.

(1932), where five people take part in
an experiment to see a year into the
future. J.B. Priestley used Dunne's theories
in his time plays, notably *Dangerous Corner*
(1932) and *Time and the Conways* (1937),
both of which consider how actions
affect the future.

Not directly influenced by Dunne
but developing the same idea are *The
World Jones Made* (1956) by Philip K. Dick,
set in a post-apocalyptic future where
Jones exists in both the present and the
near future, and *Slaughterhouse-Five* (1969)
by Kurt Vonnegut where Billy Pilgrim,
whose time sense is disjointed by his
wartime experiences, encounters the
alien Tralfamadorians, who are aware
of all time, including the end of the
universe.

Pilgrim is unstuck from time and
keeps shifting or reliving moments. In Ken
Grimwood's *Replay* (1987) the protagonist

became trapped in a time loop so that
he kept reliving his past, though with
knowledge of his former life, and each
time subtle changes occurred. Danny
Rubin used the same idea in the film
Groundhog Day (1993), where Phil Connors
is trapped within a constantly recurring
day until he can achieve the right way out.

The writer who perhaps did most to
liberate time from its regimented linearity
and take it beyond Dunne was J.G. Ballard.
He called time 'the ultimate mystery',
saying in 1980:

> Its apparently linear flux, the almost
> Renaissance perspective which
> it seems to confer on our lives,
> finally reveals itself to be part of an
> immense curvilinear system around
> which we revolve like blind drivers
> thrown onto a freeway, constantly
> passing and repassing the points in

space we have traversed an infinite
number of times before.
(from *Le Livre d'or de la science-fiction:
J.G. Ballard,* 1980)

Ballard has effectively banished
the past and future for an all-pervading
present that is wholly our own perception
and thus at the mercy of our imagination.
It is all part of, to use a term he adapted
in 1962, our 'inner space'. To Ballard, it
is not time that passes but we who pass
through time. The trappings of time are
key to almost all Ballard's fiction, but it is
at its most revealing in his short stories, all
now to be found in his *Complete Short Stories*
(2001).

Travelling through Time

There was a well-known case in 1901 when two women, Charlotte Moberly and Eleanor Jourdain, on a trip to Versailles, claimed to have found themselves back in the time of Marie Antoinette. They told their story pseudonymously as Elizabeth Morison and Frances Lamont in *An Adventure* (1911). There have been other reported cases of people 'slipping' through time, explored in *Mask of Time* (1978) by Joan Forman, but none that has yet been proved beyond doubt.

One of the earliest timeslip stories, the anonymous 'Missing One's Coach' (1838), is also written as if it were a true experience. The narrator, having missed his coach, is suddenly in eighth-century Britain with the Venerable Bede. A timeslip is an easy fictional convenience as it needs no scientific explanation. In Mark Twain's *A Connecticut Yankee in King Arthur's Court* (1889), the hero shifts back in time when he is knocked unconscious. Henry James had an old house serve as the portal in his incomplete *The Sense of the Past* (1917).

To qualify as science fiction, stories should provide some scientific rationale. For instance, in 'A Tale of the Ragged Mountains' (1844), Edgar Allan Poe uses mesmerism to account for his traveller's apparent shift to Calcutta in 1780, but leaves open a possibility of inherited memory. Jack Finney also used hypnosis in *Time and Again* (1970). In Daphne du Maurier's *The House on the Strand* (1969) it is a potent hallucinogenic drug that causes the timeslip, whilst in Audrey Niffenegger's *The Time Traveler's Wife* (2003) it is a genetic disorder. William Wallace Cook used a drug, amusingly called *tempus fugitarus*, to take his characters through time in fifty-year leaps in 'Marooned in 1492' (1905), whilst Gertrude Atherton suggested a psychic link with a distant ancestor in 'Eternal Now' (1934) – as does Octavia Butler in her powerful novel of slavery, *Kindred* (1979).

To undertake controlled time travel, a machine is essential. Journalist and future editor of the New York *Sun*, Edward Page

H.G. Wells (1866–1946)

English novelist, historian and social commentator generally regarded as the father of science fiction. A biologist and zoologist by training, his earliest stories and essays considered human evolution, such as 'The Man of the Year Million' (1893). It was thoughts on social Darwinism that prompted Wells to write *The Time Machine*, which explored the dual evolution of the capitalist elite and the socialist workers. With *The Time Machine*, Wells popularized what he called the scientific romance, which differed from the extravagant adventures of Jules Verne, by emphasizing the impact of scientific progress upon humanity in general and individuals in particular. His best-known and most influential works include *The Island of Dr Moreau* (1896), *The Invisible Man* (1897), *The War of the Worlds* (1898), *When the Sleeper Wakes* (1899), *The First Men in the Moon* (1901), *A Modern Utopia* (1905) and *The War in the Air* (1908). In these and many short stories Wells covered almost every science-fiction theme and they remain required reading.

Mitchell, was possibly the first to suggest a machine, not surprisingly a clock, in 'The Clock That Went Backward' (1881). Mitchell hints at time existing all at once and that the clock, having existed across 300 years, has the ability to travel back along its timeline. The earliest known story in which someone builds a specific time machine is 'El Anacronópete' (in *Novelas*, 1887) by Spanish diplomat and playwright Enrique Gaspar y Rimbau. Gaspar suggests that time is related to the atmosphere, as that ages everything, and his inventor, Sindulfo, creates an electric space-time machine that escapes Earth's atmosphere and flies against the Earth's rotation. He also produces a liquid that stops anyone aging or rejuvenating. The machine takes the adventurers in various leaps through history, accelerating towards the Creation.

Gaspar's work has yet to be translated into English and the credit for the first time-machine story usually goes to H.G. Wells. Wells worked on various versions of *The Time Machine* for seven years. The first, 'The Chronic Argonauts' (1888), ran as an incomplete serial and bears little comparison to the final version, but it did include Wells's speculation on time as the fourth dimension – duration, following the three spatial ones of length, breadth and thickness. Wells had probably derived this from the writings of Charles H. Hinton, collected as *Scientific Romances* (1884), which included an essay on time as the fourth dimension. Wells doggedly reworked his story till the final version appeared in 1895. It tells the story of the unnamed Time Traveller who travels to the year 802701 where humanity has split into the peaceful but naïve Eloi and their masters, the nocturnal Morlocks, who live underground. The Traveller tries to rescue the Eloi from the Morlocks but fails and only just escapes, casting his machine far into the future. He ventures 30 million years hence, seeing a dying Earth inhabited mostly by slime and crawling things.

The Time Machine was Wells's first science-fiction novel and rapidly established his name. It has generated many sequels including *Die Reise mit der Zeitmaschine* (*The Return of the Time Machine*, 1946) by Egon Friedell, *Morlock Night* (1979) by K.W. Jeter and *The Time Ships* (1995) by Stephen Baxter. Alfred Jarry wrote a surreal spoof, 'How to Build a

Time Machine' (1900), which describes a bicycle.

After Wells, the development of the time travel story was not so much in the journey, which became little more than a way of describing adventures in the future or past, but in the consequences. The ingenuity of creating or circumventing paradoxes has led to

some intriguing stories. The best known is 'By His Bootstraps' (1941) by Robert A. Heinlein. The story forms a time loop, as the protagonist finds himself moving back and forth through a time portal, meeting himself on several occasions before discovering how his future self had set the whole chain in progress. Heinlein revisited the idea in '—All You

A Sound of THUNDER

By RAY BRADBURY

They were going back sixty million years, to kill a dinosaur. And they mustn't step on one single blade of grass, or all of future civilization might be destroyed

The sign on the office wall read:

TIME SAFARI, INC.
SAFARIS TO ANY YEAR IN THE PAST
YOU NAME THE ANIMAL
WE TAKE YOU THERE
YOU SHOOT IT

Mr. Eckels smiled nervously and handed a check for ten thousand dollars to the man behind the desk.

"Does this safari guarantee I come back alive?"

"We guarantee nothing," said the official, "except the dinosaurs." He turned. "This is Mr. Travis, your Safari Guide in the Past. He'll tell you what and where to shoot. If he says no shooting, no shooting. If you don't follow directions, there's a stiff penalty of another ten thousand dollars, plus possible government action, on your return."

Eckels looked across the vast office at an arrangement of wires, golden boxes and an aurora that flickered like a great bonfire.

"Hell and damn," Eckels breathed, the light of the Machine on his thin face. "A real time machine." He shook his head. "Makes you think. If the election had gone badly yesterday, I might be here now running away from the results. Thank God Keith won. He'll make a fine President of the United States."

"Yes," said the man behind the desk. "We're lucky. If Lyman had gotten in, we'd have the worst kind of dictatorship. There's an anti-everything man for you—a militarist, anti-Christ, anti-human, anti-intellectual. People called us up, you know, joking but not joking. Said if Lyman got elected they wanted to go live in 1492. Of course, it's not our business to conduct escapes, but to form safaris. Anyway, Keith's President now. All you got to worry about is—"

"Shooting my dinosaur," Eckels said.

"A Tyrannosaurus rex. The damnedest monster in history. Sign this release. Anything happens to you, we're not responsible. Those dinosaurs are hungry."

Eckels flushed angrily. "Trying to scare me!"

"Frankly, yes. We don't want anyone going who'll panic at the first shot. Six safari leaders were killed last year, and a dozen hunters. We're here to give you the damnedest thrill a *real* hunter ever asked for. Taking you back sixty million years to bag the biggest damned game in all time. Your personal check's still there. Tear it up."

Mr. Eckels looked at the check for a long time. His fingers twitched.

"Good luck," said the man behind the desk. "Mr. Travis, he's all yours."

They moved silently across the room, taking their guns with them, toward the Machine, toward the silver metal and the roaring light. . . .

First a day and then a night and then a day and

then a night, then it was day-night-day-night-day. A week, a month, a year, a decade! 2056 A.D., 2019 A.D., 1999! 1957! Gone! The Machine roared.

They put on their oxygen helmets and tested the intercoms.

Eckels swayed on the padded seat, his face pale, his jaw stiff. He felt the trembling in his arms, and he looked down and found his hands tight on the new rifle. There were four other men in the Machine: Travis, the safari leader; his assistant, Lesperance; and two other hunters, Billings and Kramer. They sat looking at one another, and the years blazed around them.

"Can these guns get a dinosaur cold?" Eckels felt his mouth saying.

"If you hit them right," Travis said on the helmet radio. "Some dinosaurs have the equivalent of two brains, one in the head, another—a nerve plexus—far down the spinal column. We stay away from those. That's stretching luck. Put your first two shots into the eyes, if you can—blind them and go back into the brain."

THE Machine howled. Time was a film run backward. Suns fled and ten million moons fled after them. "Good God," said Eckels. "Every hunter that ever lived would envy us today. This makes Africa seem like Illinois."

The Machine slowed; its scream fell to a murmur. The Machine stopped.

The sun stopped in the sky.

The fog that had enveloped the Machine blew away, and they were in an old time, a very old time indeed, three hunters and two safari heads with their blue metal guns across their knees.

"Christ isn't born yet," said Travis, "Moses has not gone to the mountain to talk with God. The Pyramids are still in the earth, waiting to be cut out and put up. *Remember* that. Alexander, Caesar, Napoleon, Hitler—none of them exists."

The men nodded.

"That," Mr. Travis said, pointing, "is the jungle of sixty million two thousand and fifty-five years before President Keith."

He indicated a metal path that wandered into green wilderness, over steaming swamp, among giant ferns and palms.

"And that," he said, "is the Path, laid by Time Safari for your use. It floats six inches above the earth. Doesn't touch so much as one grass blade, flower or tree. It's an antigravity metal. Its purpose is to keep you from touching this world of the past in any way. Stay *(Continued on page 60)*

The monster lunged forward with a terrible scream. The rifles jerked up and blazed fire. The great reptile's tail lashed sideways

Collier's for June 28,

ILLUSTRATED BY FREDERICK SIEBEL

Ray Bradbury's 'A Sound of
Thunder', first published in
Collier's Weekly, 28 June 1952,
illustrated by Frederick Siebel.
A53 NPL

Just imagine. You're allowed
one trip only through time. Would you
choose the past or the future, and to
when would you go? And why?

Zombies–'(1959), where the time loop
doubles again so that all the characters
are the same individual including being
his/her own mother and father. David
Gerrold reworked the same idea in the
highly convoluted *The Man Who Folded Himself*
(1973). The idea of trying to influence
your past self may prove bittersweet, as
the polarizing moment proved in Osbert
Sitwell's *The Man Who Lost Himself* (1929).

The ultimate paradox for the time
traveller is what might happen if you go
back and kill your father or grandfather
before you are conceived? This was
first explored by Nathan Schachner in
'Ancestral Voices' (1933), written to
highlight how multiracial the population
had become. His protagonist goes back
in time and kills a Hun with the result
that millions of people all over the world
vanish. In *Le Voyageur imprudent* (The Careless
Traveller, 1944; trans. as *Future Times Three*,
1958) René Barjavel has his hero go
back to assassinate the young Napoleon
Bonaparte, but by mistake kills his own
grandfather and thus eliminates himself.

One of the most extreme stories
about changing the past is 'Un Brillant
Sujet' ('A Brilliant Topic', 1922) by Jacques
Rigaut in which a man determines to
readjust Western fundamental beliefs
by affecting every key event in history,
including killing the Christ child. Ray
Bradbury penned what many believe is
the definitive story on how the present
depends on the past in 'A Sound of
Thunder' (1952), in which a traveller
inadvertently steps on a butterfly
during the age of the dinosaurs and
back in the present discovers a number
of subtle but disturbing changes.

Perhaps the past is immutable
and cannot be changed. Lewis Carroll
wondered that in *Sylvie and Bruno* (1889).
He describes an 'outlandish' watch that
can be turned to revert to a previous
moment. When the Professor uses it to
try and prevent an accident (a crashed
bicycle) he succeeds, but only for the
accident to happen another way. The
inevitability of events is explored in 'Try
and Change the Past' (1958) by Fritz
Leiber and 'The Men Who Murdered
Mohammed' (1958) by Alfred Bester.
It is a critical part of *Flashforward* (1999)
by Robert J. Sawyer, which questions to
what extent events are predestined. In her

Left Cover of Gaspar's *Novelas*
(1887) for 'El Anacronópete'
depicting the earliest known
portrayal of a time machine.
RB.23.a.34806

Above Hubert Rogers's cover
for *Astounding*, October 1941,
featuring 'By His Bootstraps'
by Robert A. Heinlein
(as Anson McDonald).

Right Interior of the Tardis from
Dr Who.

various time-travel novels Connie Willis
shows how the past protects itself by
healing itself or diverting time travellers.
However, in *Doomsday Book* (1992) and *To
Say Nothing of the Dog* (1997), where the past
is explored purely for research purposes
by historians from Oxford University,
time's way of correcting itself does not
always lead to the expected outcome.

In order that history is protected it
may be necessary to police time or fight
to secure a certain timeline. The seminal
novel is *The Legion of Time* (1938) by Jack
Williamson in which two crucial timelines
depend upon whether a boy, John Barr,

picks up a magnet or a stone. The two
distinct worlds that arise compete to
ensure his action favours their timeline.
It was from this story that the phrase
'Jonbar Point' was coined by Brian W.
Aldiss in 1964 to suggest any critical event
upon which differing futures depend.
Keeping Sarah Connor alive is the Jonbar
Point in the first *Terminator* (1984) film.

Protecting the timelines is one of
the roles of the Time Lords of which
the Doctor in *Dr Who* is the best known.
Created by Sydney Newman and Donald
Wilson for the BBC in 1963, *Dr Who*
is now the longest-running television

science-fiction series in the world. The Doctor's time machine, the TARDIS ('Time and Relative Dimensions in Space') was supposed to change appearance to blend in with local surroundings, but had malfunctioned and was stuck as a 1950s-style police phone box. The name has passed into the language to describe anything that appears bigger on the inside than the outside.

In *Dr Who*, protecting the timelines often leads to conflict and there are many novels of different timelines scheming to protect themselves or the integrity of a primary line. These include *The End of Eternity* (1955) by Isaac Asimov, *Time Patrol* (1960) by Poul Anderson, *The Fall of Chronopolis* (1974) by Barrington J. Bayley, *Destiny Times Three* (1945) and *The Change War* (1978) by Fritz Leiber, 'The Great Work of Time' (1989) by John Crowley (where a secret society does its best to ensure that our existing timeline does not happen) and, amongst the most complicated, with many timelines and paradoxes, *Dinosaur Beach* (1971) by Keith Laumer and *Cowl* (2004) by Neal Asher.

All of which raises the question of how the world may have changed had the past been different.

Failure to control the timelines can lead to alternate histories, sometimes called uchronia or counterfactuals, a theme that fascinates historians as much as it does science-fiction writers. Niall Ferguson compiled a collection of essays, *Virtual History* (1997), with such contributions as 'England without Cromwell' and 'Hitler's England'. A similar volume, *If It Had Happened Otherwise* (1931), had been compiled by J.C. Squire over sixty years earlier and included Sir Winston Churchill with 'If Lee Had not Won the Battle of Gettysburg' and Harold Nicolson on 'If Byron had become King of Greece'.

Speculation about how things might otherwise have happened dates back to Roman times. In *Ab urbe condita* (From the Founding of the City, *c.*25BC), Livy wondered what might have happened had Alexander the Great expanded his empire westward towards Rome.

The earliest known alternate history novel is *Napoléon et la conquête du monde* (1836) by Louis-Napoléon Geoffroy-Château in which Napoleon defeats Russia, invades Britain and becomes emperor of the world. Edward Everett Hale went further back into history and in 'Hands Off' (1881) considered what might have happened

had Joseph not been sold into slavery in Egypt, which leads to the rise of a Phoenician empire. *Aristopia* (1895) by Castello Holford looked at the emergence of a different North America following the discovery of gold in Virginia.

Murray Leinster's 'Sidewise in Time' (1934) introduced alternate worlds to pulp science fiction by having a series of timeshifts make the Earth a patchwork of alternities. Most writers, however, have considered one significant event and extrapolated the consequences. Vasily Aksenov's *Ostrov Krym* (*The Island of Crimea*, 1979) describes how the White Guard were able to defend the Crimea, because it was an island not a peninsula, and as a result Crimea became an independent state and not part of the Soviet Union. The book was banned in Russia and Aksenov stripped of his Russian citizenship.

One of the earliest Jonbar Points takes us back some 65 million years when, in *West of Eden* (1984), Harry Harrison reveals that the dinosaurs did not become extinct but continued to evolve. Likewise in *The Malacia Tapestry* (1976) Brian Aldiss has the equivalent of mankind descended from the dinosaurs. Here is a selection of less distant Jonbar Points.

Above Cover of F&SF, November 1952, by Ed Emshwiller, illustrating *Bring the Jubilee* by Ward Moore.
P.P.6383.agz

Right In 1978 the British magazine *New Worlds* presented its contents as an alternate-world newspaper. This front page of the *Guardian* for 20 May 1948 was devised by the editor Michael Moorcock.

Jesus is not crucified and Christianity does not develop	*Ponce Pilate* (1961), Roger Caillois; *The Last Starship from Earth* (1968), John Boyd; *A World Unknown* (1975), John Clagett; *Procurator* (1984), Kirk Mitchell
Roman Empire did not fall	*Fireball* (1981), John Christopher; *The Aquiliad* (1983), S.P. Somtow; *Roma Eterna* (2003), Robert Silverberg; *Romanitas* (2005), Sophia McDougall
William of Normandy loses the Battle of Hastings	*Timeswitch* (2009), John Gribbin
The Black Death was even more virulent	*The Gate of Worlds* (1967), Robert Silverberg; *The Years of Rice and Salt* (2002), Kim Stanley Robinson; *In High Places* (2006), Harry Turtledove
The Spanish Armada was victorious	*Times Without Number* (1962), John Brunner; *Pavane* (1968), Keith Roberts; *Shadow of Earth* (1979), Phyllis Eisenstein; *Un día de gloria* (2001), Javier González
The South won the American Civil War	*Bring the Jubilee* (1953), Ward Moore; *The Wild Blue and the Gray* (1991) William Sanders; *How Few Remain* (1997), Harry Turtledove
Germany won World War I	*Worlds of the Imperium* (1962), Keith Laumer; *Si les Allemands avaient gagné la guerre* (1921), Gaston Homsy; *Curious Notions* (2004), Harry Turtledove; *The Summer Isles* (2005), Ian MacLeod
Germany won World War II	*Mi, I. Adolf* (1945), László Gáspár; *The Sound of His Horn* (1952), Sarban (John W. Wall); *The Man in the High Castle* (1962), Philip K. Dick; *SS-GB* (1978), Len Deighton; *Cette Terre* (1981), Michel Jeury; *Fatherland* (1992), Robert Harris; *Making History* (1996), Stephen Fry; *Peklo Beneš* (Benes Hell, 2002), Josef Nesvadba
President Kennedy was not assassinated	*Fortress* (1987), David Drake; *The Man Who Turned Into Himself* (1993), David Ambrose; *It Rained in Dallas* (2002), Robert Rienzi; *In War Times* (2007), Kathleen Ann Goonan

THE GUARDIAN

Toronto   Tuesday May 20 1948

Crossman leads attack on Kremlin

By ROY KIPLING

There was still fierce fighting in the streets of Moscow today as General Sir Richard Crossman led a massive hovertank charge against the Kremlin where most of the Duma forces are now entrenched.

Earlier, a mixed division of British and Hungarian troops was able to reach Lubyanka Prison and release Emperor Michael and his family. They were unhurt. So far no press interviews have been granted. Much of the city is in ruins and already the outskirts are under military law. Meanwhile a minor sensation was created when a neutral Dutch war-correspondent, Jeremiah Cornelius, was discovered to be a double agent. He was shot this morning at the orders of the Israeli Commander Field Marshal Dayan. Israeli troops now occupy the whole of the the southern section of the city and are proving, it is said, uncooperative with the other allied forces. In a statement issued yesterday evening, General Crossman said that he was confident that the Kremlin would fall by today.

(Victims of Ideology p.7)

German rift with soviet French

From OSWALD BASTABLE

Signs that the Franco-German Soviet Bloc is suffering internal disruptions were confirmed (say Versailles-watchers) by the announcement that Hugo Pyat had been replaced as leader of the Assembly by known hardliner Otto Lobkovitz. Lobkovitz, an Alsatian, is likely to have more success at reconciling differences between German and French members of the Assembly. These differences came to a head last month when the Ministry of Agriculture demanded that productivity on the Rhine collectives be doubled within three years. This was regarded by Germans as a French attempt to make up for their own poor agricultural returns in the past two years. While Lobkovitz may heal the rift within the Assembly concerning the agricultural issue, he will almost certainly bring up the Polish question at his first opportunity, with a consequent further increase in tension between the two factions.

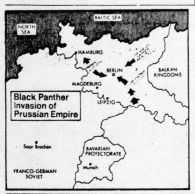

Black Panther Invasion of Prussian Empire

Panthers speed on Berlin

The mood in Berlin today was, to say the least, gloomy as the news reached the Prussian capital of further Black Panther games in nearby towns. The remains of the Prussian army has retreated to Berlin and is now under the direct command of President-Emperor Manfred von Bismark. In a series of brilliant manoeuvres Black Panther armoured divisions have smashed through all other defences and are now moving rapidly on the capital. BP C-in-C General Seale claimed this morning that by tomorrow he would be 'dining in the Chancery'. The Prussian surrender is expected at any moment.

(Bohemia Next? Back Page)

British Jews face dole queues

JAMES COLVIN

If the new Alien Registration Bill becomes law after the House of Commons votes on Friday many British Jews will find themselves suddenly unemployed, said the Liberal Shadow Minister for Race Control, Dr Mark Bonham Carter, yesterday. In a speech to his constituency party at Haringay W, he told a packed hall that the Bill would not only control Jewish immigration into this country but would make it impossible for many British-born Jews to qualify for jobs. 'Unless the Bill is modified', he said, 'people who are entitled to regard themselves as British subjects will face the prospect of the dole queue or, at best, performing menial work when they have previously been practising in the professions or in the better-rewarded branches of trade and industry.' He said that Liberals were not opposed to the basic spirit of the Bill but would vote against it unless it was modified to protect British Nationals.

Iceland's military image left in ruins

By MEG ZETTERLING

Reykjavik, Monday

The ease with which a relatively small force of Swedish paratroopers were able to regain control of the country after Prime Minister Christiansen's announcement on Friday of his country's 'independence' has left Iceland's previously impressive military image in complete ruins. The hopes of various terrorist organisations in Norway, Denmark and Finland (so called 'Liberation Armies') must have been sadly dashed when it took the Swedes only a matter of hours to re-establish law and order throughout Iceland. Many had previously been of the opinion that the 'Swedish wolverine' had let its teeth decay but Sunday's show of superior strength, speed and tactical ability will have squashed that impression for once and for all. This morning President Hellander told the Swedish Parliament that he was 'completely satisfied' with the manner in which the Icelandic 'uprising' had been dealt.

(Alan Brien, p.12)

TV, radio—2

Arts 12	Overseas . 2-4
Books 24, 25	Parliament 20
Business 17-19	Sport . 25, 27
Ent'ments 20	Women ... 11
Home... 5-8	X-words 23, 27
Horner ... 9	

Classified —

9, 10, 21-23

Surprising end to a strange week

Gandhi avenges his earlier torment

By HOPE DEMPSEY

In a week which saw three separate assassination attempts on the life of President Gandhi of Bantustan (formerly Cape Colony), and in which it seemed inevitable that the death for alleged treason. The Indian-born dictator must surely five leaders are F W Waring (Natfall, it has become obvious that ional Democrat), B J Vorster the President is now even more (Christian Republican), A Luthfirmly in control than before. uli (Bantu Nationalist), K Man-

The so called 'minority' parties have been declared illegal and sentenced five 'minority' leaders to tamzima (South African Unity) and H Cornelius (Liberal). In some circles here Gandhi's severe sentences are seen as vengeance on the representatives of those who were originally responsible for his fifteen years of imprisonment, exile and, according to his own statements, torture while interned in the Capetown Correction Centre.

One form of alternate history that has become a category of its own is steampunk. It supposes that the Victorian and Edwardian science-fiction writers were correct and their visions came true, so that the world is filled with enhanced late Victorian or Edwardian technology: airships, vast calculating machines, automatons. The British Empire still exists, and adventurers sit in their rich leather chairs in their clubs in London and Paris and plan how they will travel/save/conquer the world. It is the world of Jules Verne, H.G. Wells and Sherlock Holmes projected into an alternate Victorian future.

The word itself was coined by K.W. Jeter in 1987 as a facetious extension from 'cyberpunk' to categorize his book *Morlock Night* (1979) in which the Morlocks of H.G. Wells's *Time Machine* killed the Time Traveller on his return visit and used the machine to return to Victorian London. Although Jeter defined the genre, there were earlier examples. Joan Aiken's *The Wolves of Willoughby Chase* (1962) and sequels are set in a genuine alternate Britain where the Hanoverian succession never happened and the Jacobites regained the throne. Steam-powered technology has thrived including the construction of a Channel Tunnel. The success of the book led to a long series, which became increasingly full of proto-steampunk imagery. Michael Moorcock's *The Warlord of the Air* (1971), the first of his Oswald Bastable novels, is set in an Edwardian British Empire where World War I never happened and airships are dominant. Also of importance is Harry Harrison's *A Transatlantic Tunnel, Hurrah!* (1973), set in an alternate 1973 where the British Empire is dominant and still retains the American colonies, and where technology still boasts Victorian vigour.

Amongst Jeter's circle of writers were Tim Powers and James P. Blaylock, both of whom turned to steampunk.

Powers's *The Anubis Gates* (1983), although a fantasy, did much to stir up interest in the imagery of early nineteenth-century London and the machinations of secret societies. Although Blaylock's *The Digging Leviathan* (1984), is set in 1964 it involves a group of scientists who use pulp- and Victorian-style technology to create a machine capable of boring to the centre of the Earth. Blaylock went the whole hog in two sequels, *Homunculus* (1986) and *Lord Kelvin's Machine* (1992), both set in Victorian England and both involving unusual technologies.

The book that did most to raise public awareness to steampunk was *The Difference Engine* (1990) by William Gibson and Bruce Sterling, which describes an alternate mid-Victorian England, in which Byron still lived, and where Charles Babbage's Difference Engine and Analytical Engine had become commercially viable, leading to a steam-driven internet. Paul Di Filippo added much humour to the genre and exported steampunk to the American streets in the novellas that make up *The Steampunk Trilogy* (1995).

Alan Moore's *The League of Extraordinary Gentlemen* comic-book series, which began in 1999 and illustrated by Kevin O'Neill, added new vigour to steampunk. He brought together various literary heroes, such as Allan Quatermain, Captain Nemo and Mycroft Holmes, who use their own astonishing inventions, such as Nemo's *Nautilus* submarine to combat other literary villains – such as Fu Manchu and Wells's Martian invaders.

Steampunk is closer to fantasy than science fiction, but has fun with the concepts of futures as well as pasts that might have been. The field has already spread and fragmented and created a dedicated following, delighting in worlds of scientific romance, nostalgia and wonders that almost but never were.

'The Angel of Goliad' by William Gibson and Bruce Sterling, the first appearance of an excerpt from *The Difference Engine* run in *Interzone*, October 1990, illustration by Ian Miller.
P.903/835

Right *The League of Extraordinary Gentlemen* (1999) by Alan Moore, with Captain Nemo's *Nautilus*, illustration by Kevin O'Neill.
DC comics.
YK.2204.b.1898

Parallel Worlds

If we can pass from our own world to an alternate world, where history has taken a different path, might there not be other worlds parallel to our own, but not related to our world? These worlds are usually thought of as occupying another dimension, where the world exists alongside ours but is invisible to our eyes because we can only see the three spatial dimensions. These might be the fourth or fifth dimension, though in higher mathematics there can be an infinite number of dimensions. Topological experiments have extrapolated a fourth-dimensional tesseract from a three-dimensional cube.

The word, spelled as 'tessaract', was coined by Charles H. Hinton in *A New Era of Thought* (1888), a book that was influential not only on fiction but also on various philosophical and theosophical organizations, by way of explaining spiritual and astral planes. One of Hinton's colleagues was educationalist Edwin A. Abbott, author of a quirky little book, *Flatland* (1884). Flatland is a two-dimensional world and the story, narrated by 'A. Square', explores one-dimensional beings who have no comprehension of a two-dimensional world, and a three-dimensional being that can only partly be seen in two dimensions.

The idea that there may be other dimensional beings around us only partially visible in certain circumstances is central to 'Un Autre Monde' (1895) by J.-H. Rosny and 'The Plattner Story' (1896) by H.G. Wells. Algernon Blackwood, best known for his supernatural fiction, was fascinated with the concept of other dimensions, which he called higher space. It features in several stories, notably 'The Willows' (1907), where travellers camping on an isolated river island find they are at a vortex between this world and another. Two early classics of pulp fiction – *The Heads of Cerberus* (1919; book, 1952) by Francis Stevens and *The Blind Spot* (1921; book, 1951) by Austin Hall and Homer Eon Flint – both suggest that parallel worlds exist alongside ours at a different 'vibratory rate', a concept latched onto by many writers as easier to understand than higher mathematics.

Edwin A. Abbott's own design for the title page of *Flatland* (1884) here shown in a 1950 reprint.

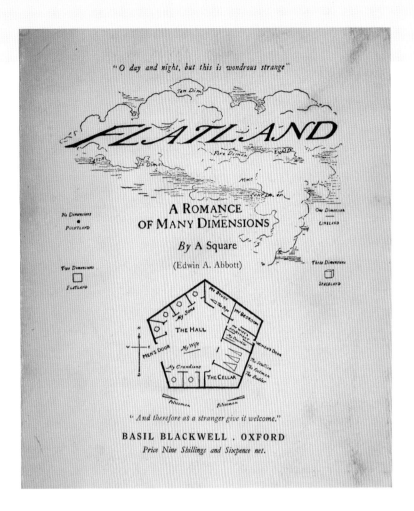

Left 'The Bridge Between the Worlds' from *Un Autre Monde* (1844) by J. J. Grandville, which describes a parallel world full of strange anthropomorphic beings.

Michael Moorcock (born 1939)

English novelist, storywriter and magazine editor, renowned in science fiction as the champion of the New Wave movement in the mid-1960s through his editorship of *New Worlds*. Early in his career Moorcock introduced the concept of the Multiverse in *The Sundered Worlds* (1962; book, 1965; also as *The Blood-Red Game*). The universe is contracting and mankind seeks to escape by moving into another part of the Multiverse, which is a series of parallel universes that overlap at points. Most of Moorcock's novels and stories take place in one or more aspects of the Multiverse. Many of his major characters are different manifestations of the Eternal Champion, who fights to achieve a cosmic balance in the constant battle between the forces of Law and Chaos. The most famous aspect of the Champion is Elric of Melniboné, an albino prince who is spiritually bonded with his demon sword, Stormbringer. Others include fantasy heroes, such as Dorian Hawkmoon, Corum and Erekosë, as well as science-fiction characters Jerry Cornelius, Jherek Carnelian and Oswald Bastable. Moorcock wrote several novels where chapters overlap between books so that the same events happen viewed from a different character's perspective, as will be found in *The Sleeping Sorceress* (1971; also as *The Vanishing Tower*) with *The King of the Swords* (1971) and *The Quest for Tanelorn* (1975) with *The Sailor on the Seas of Fate* (1976). Of his other books, *Behold the Man* (1969) is a powerful study of an obsessed man who travels back in time to meet Jesus but, discovering the real Jesus is mentally deficient, takes on the role himself. Moorcock is fascinated with the end of time and explores its ultimate decadence in his Dancers at the End of Time sequence that began with *An Alien Heat* (1972).

The omnibus edition of *The Dancers at the End of Time* (1981), cover by Rodney Matthews.
X.950/4306

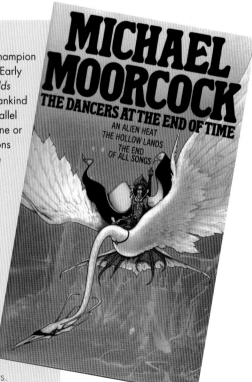

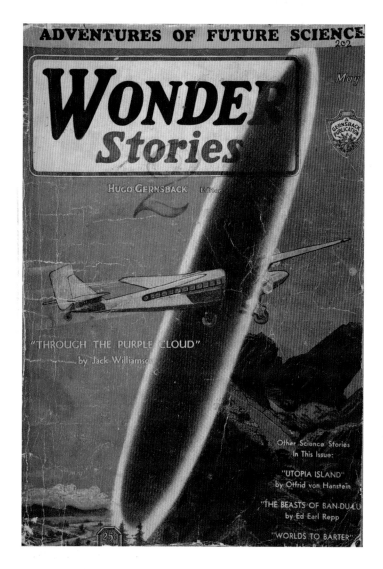

ADVENTURES OF FUTURE SCIENCE

In 1858 the German mathematician August Möbius demonstrated how you can manipulate the dimensions by twisting a strip of paper so that it has only one side. Martin Gardner went further in 'The No-Sided Professor' (1946) to have a paper with no sides at all, an idea also used by Ian McEwan in 'Solid Geometry' (1975).

Writers were fascinated by the idea of vanishing points within an interface of dimensions. Fitz-James O'Brien set 'The Lost Room' (1858) in a house with a maze of corridors that seem to defy mathematics. 'The Hall Bedroom' (1903) by Mary Wilkins Freeman is about a room larger at night than during the day and from where the occupant disappears. Robert A. Heinlein resurrected the idea in '"—And He Built a Crooked House—"' (1941), where an architect builds a house in the form of a tesseract that, when jolted by an earthquake, folds in on

itself. A.J. Deutsch also had fun with 'A Subway Named Möbius' (1950), where Boston's new underground system is so complicated that a train vanishes between the dimensions. More recently in 'The Eighth Room' (1989), Stephen Baxter has what is left of the human race locked in an area of hyperspace accessible only via a hypercube.

Travelling to another dimension was more convenient in fiction than travelling through space as it could happen in an instant. In 'The City of Singing Flame' (1931), Clark Ashton Smith has a writer pass through a portal into an exotic land lured by the seductive sound of a singing flame. Smith wrote several stories of other dimensions of which the most unusual was 'The Dimension of Chance' (1932), depicting a world of randomness with no uniformity as if it were all the pieces left over from the world. Both this story and

Above left *Wonder Stories*, May 1931, with Frank R. Paul's illustration for 'Through the Purple Cloud' by Jack Williamson.

Above *Wonder Stories*, July 1931, with Frank R. Paul's illustration for 'The City of Singing Flame' by Clark Ashton Smith.

Isaac Asimov HOW LITTLE!

THE MAGAZINE OF
Fantasy & Science Fiction
SEPTEMBER

Joanna Russ   William Walling
Bob Leman   Gary Jennings

09 $1.25
UK 75p

Ron Walotsky's cover for *The Magazine of Fantasy & Science Fiction,* September 1979, depicting a portal to other worlds from 'The Extraordinary Voyages of Amélie Bertrand' by Joanna Russ.

P.P.6383.agz

Just imagine. Create your own Möbius strip. Take a thin strip of paper, twist it just once and join the ends together. Draw a line along the centre from any starting point till you return to that point. You'll find the line is on both sides of the paper! What happens if you cut along that line?

Jack Williamson's 'Through the Purple Cloud' (1931), have a plane fly through a mist into an alien world, not unlike the aircraft that vanish in the Bermuda Triangle, outlined in Vincent Gaddis's *Invisible Horizons* (1965).

One of the most enchanting of all trans-dimensional stories is 'Mimsy Were the Borogoves' (1943) by Henry Kuttner and Catherine Moore, writing as Lewis Padgett. In the far future a scientist sends various toys back into the past. They arrive at two different times. One batch is found by Alice Liddell, the original Alice in Wonderland, who does not understand the toys but passes details on to Lewis Carroll, who incorporates the title phrase into his poem 'Jabberwocky'. This is read a century later by the children who found the other batch of toys and who learned from them how to cross the dimensions. Uttering

the words from 'Jabberwocky', they 'went in a direction [their father] could not understand.'

The variety of other-dimension stories, whether as a mathematical concept or as a parallel world, is extensive. At one end is the 'bottomless pit' idea, where access to another dimension allows either a seemingly inexhaustible supply of items, as in 'Tiger by the Tail' (1951) by Alan E. Nourse, or a solution to waste disposal, as in 'Dusty Zebra' (1954) by Clifford D. Simak. Isaac Asimov took this to an extreme in *The Gods Themselves* (1972), where an energy exchange between two parallel universes threatens to destroy our own.

At the other end is the concept of the Multiverse, a whole series of parallel universes. This idea has most famously been used by Michael Moorcock for his Eternal Champion stories, where various aspects of the Champion exist in and occasionally interact across the many worlds. Clifford D. Simak had earlier proposed the idea for an infinite number of Earths in *Ring Around the Sun* (1953). Robert A. Heinlein parodied the concept in *The Number of the Beast* (1980), where he has a six-dimensional spaceship that allows access to the dimensions of fiction. According to the theoretical physicist Michio Kaku the existence of parallel universes can be proved, which he reveals (via M-theory) in his *Parallel Worlds* (2005).

Between these two extremes are stories that explore the interraction between our dimension and another. Joseph Conrad helped his friend Ford Madox Hueffer complete *The Inheritors* (1901), a novel primarily of social and political comment but anticipating that life on Earth would one day be superseded by beings from another dimension, the Dimensionists, who lack all human scruples and represent the future. H.G. Wells, on the other hand, believed, in *Men Like Gods* (1923), that beings in a parallel world are vastly superior to humans and that contact with them (which happens by accident) will enhance human life.

The fascination for parallel worlds is that there may well be another world alongside ours, perhaps more aware of us than we are of it, and that maybe just now and then we can interract. It is the idea of infinite possibilities.

Virtual Worlds

Besides parallel worlds and alternate histories, there may be other worlds we can perceive that are much closer. Let us not forget the power of our imagination, whether controlled or uncontrolled. Where do we go in our dreams? Is it possible, with developments in psychoanalysis and our understanding of the brain, for someone to enter or experience someone else's dream-world? And if so, how do we know whether we are in the real world or are only dreaming? Maybe we are the figment of somebody else's dream.

The French philosopher René Descartes gave this much thought in his *Meditationes de prima philosophia* (1641), the work that included his famous quote usually rendered as 'I think, therefore I am.' He raised the solipsist dilemma that we can only know as much of the world as we perceive in our mind and this may lead to confusion between reality and imagination. Indeed, what is reality? Do we know that the world about us exists as we see it, or is it a fabrication created for our own existence as depicted in *The Matrix* films?

Until the advent of computers and virtual reality we might have dismissed this as a philosophical argument, but the emergence of cyberspace, the possibility of 'inhabiting' a computer-created virtual reality, provides a scientific basis that propels the concept into the world of science fiction, and raises a genuine ontological debate. Does the world out there exist as we believe or will it suddenly be revealed, as in the film *The Truman Show* (1998), as a fabrication? Are our minds our own or are we being controlled by others? And are these others human, or alien, or are we no more than a computer simulation?

Ironically, the very first use of the phrase 'science fiction' was to describe a book about perception. Writing in *A Little Earnest Book upon a Great Old Subject* (1851), William Wilson referred to R.H. Horne's *The Poor Artist* (1850), in which an artist paints a coin in seven different ways as perceived by seven different creatures, as an example of 'science fiction'. It might not fit the definition we use today, but the fact that different creatures, and different people, perceive the same thing in a multitude of ways, challenges perception and reality. How do we know whether what we see is the same as what anyone else sees, and how do we know which is correct?

Then there is the question of the power of the mind. How much do we understand the abilities of our mind, or our psyche? Are telepathy, telekinesis and other psychic powers really in the realms of fantasy, or a science as yet unexplored?

All of these thoughts bring us to the ultimate in paranoia, questioning everything in the world and believing everything is a conspiracy. Paranoia, reality, dream-worlds, cyberspace and the power of the mind – all are the subject of this section.

Right The Cyberworld of *The Matrix* (1999), written and directed by Larry and Andy Wachowski.

Worlds of the Mind

There are two lives to each of us, gliding on at the same time, scarcely connected with each other — the life of our actions, the life of our minds; the external and the inward history...

So wrote Edward Bulwer (later Lord Lytton) in an episode in *The Pilgrims of the Rhine* (1834) where a man lives in his own dream-world. It raises the question of whether our mind, through the power of our imagination, is sufficient to create a separate life.

In *Through the Looking-Glass, and what Alice Found There* (1871), Lewis Carroll has Tweedledum and Tweedledee show Alice where the Red King is sleeping and remark that Alice exists only in his dreams and that if he woke she would puff out like a candle.

Mark Twain, best known for *Tom Sawyer*, was fascinated by the idea of the real self and the dream self. At the same time that Sigmund Freud was developing his theories of the subconscious, part of which would emerge in *Die Traumdeutung* (1899; as *The Interpretation of Dreams*, 1913), Twain was struggling to work his ideas into fiction. In 1898 he began but never finished a novella, posthumously entitled 'The Great Dark' (1966), where the Superintendent of Dreams offers a man a voyage in a ship on a drop of water that the man had been studying through a microscope. The man finds himself on the ship with his family and is told that this is his real life and the earlier memory was a dream, but later realizes he is trapped in a nightmare. In 'The Mysterious Stranger' (1916), written about the same time in several versions, the narrator finds that various problems he has encountered are all an illusion and that nothing exists beyond his imagination. In 'My Platonic Sweetheart' (1912) the narrator has a recurring dream in which he meets a young woman, though in each dream they both have different identities.

Journeys into our dream-worlds are often allegories, as in one of the most famous, *The Pilgrim's Progress* (1678–84)

LOOKING-GLASS HOUSE.   11

there. And certainly the glass *was* beginning to melt away, just like a bright silvery mist.

In another moment Alice was through the

by John Bunyan. This is 'delivered under the similitude of a dream' and follows Christian through the trials of this life into the next within an allegorical landscape. George MacDonald, a close friend of Lewis Carroll, wrote a dark parallel to *The Pilgrim's Progress* in *Lilith* (1895). His character, Vane, enters another world via a mirror where he is given the chance of salvation via rebirth but refuses, and as a consequence has a series of doomed wanderings. In a similar vein is David Lindsay's *A Voyage to Arcturus* (1920), which though not a dream-world bears the same allegorical hallmarks. Maskull finds himself on the planet Tormance where he is reborn and faces various challenges. H.P. Lovecraft's stories featuring Randolph Carter, notably 'Through the Gates of the Silver Key' (1934) and 'The Dream-Quest of Unknown Kadath' (1943), show clearly the dual lives in dream and non-dream as suggested by Bulwer.

Writers may go to great lengths in developing their characters and settings. The Brontë children became obsessive

Left Alice passes into Looking-Glass land in *Through the Looking-Glass* (1871) by Lewis Carroll, illustrated by John Tenniel.
C.71.b.33

Right The *Codex Seraphinianus*, first published in 1981, is the work of Italian artist and designer Luigi Serafini and is a compendium, like a natural history, of an unknown world. The images conjure up thoughts ranging from Hieronymus Bosch to M.C. Escher and the language reminds one of *The Voynich Manuscript*, now dated to the early fifteenth century, both being indecipherable and incomprehensible. *The Codex* is a beautiful example of a complete yet inaccessible world of the imagination.
LB.31.c.1219

about their imaginary worlds, Angria and Gondal, drawing maps and creating lives for their characters. The stories are in tiny micro-script, as if written by their miniature toy soldiers. This was unusual for their time, though it has become more common today for fictional worlds to be elaborate, especially since the work of J.R.R. Tolkien in creating Middle Earth. This has in turn led to role-playing games and shared worlds where players can become part of their fantasy world.

There are many precedents for immersion in fantasy worlds. As far back as 1850, in 'La Lunette de Hans Schnaps', Emile Erckmann and Alexandre Chatrian used the idea of a specially adapted kaleidoscope to capture and display the viewer's desires and dreams. In 'The Ultimate Adventure' (1939), L. Ron Hubbard, renowned as the creator of Scientology, has a research scientist use sensory deprivation techniques to send a man into the world of the Arabian Nights. Hubbard reworked the idea in 'Typewriter in the Sky' (1940) where an author uses a friend as a character in a novel, and the friend finds himself at the mercy of the writer, fighting for his own survival. Robert Bloch, best known as the author of *Psycho* (1959), has a psychiatrist take his patients into their literary dream-worlds in 'All on a Golden Afternoon' (1956), whilst in 'The Plot is the Thing' (1966) a woman becomes so obsessed with her favourite TV programmes that she finds herself in them.

Despite the psychological element, most of these stories are treated as fantasy and the extent to which the mind might possess psychic powers remains subject to scientific research. In 'Father of Lies' (1962; book, 1968), John Brunner has a traveller enter a fantasy world that he subsequently discovers has been created entirely by psychic projection by a young boy. Haruki Murakami's 1985 novel *Sekai no owari to hādo-boirudo wandārando* (*Hard-Boiled Wonderland and the End of the World*) features a character whose brain is used as a computer and who creates his own populated walled city in his subconscious. Ursula K. Le Guin took the idea to extremes in *The Lathe of Heaven* (1971) in which a man, George Orr, is

The map by Branwell Brontë of Glass Town, Angria from his and Charlotte's notebooks.
Ashley Ms.2468 f.1b

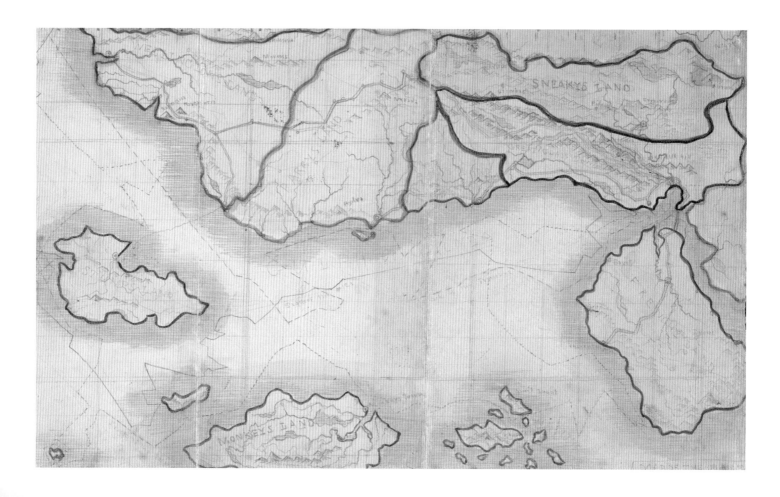

Christopher Priest (born 1943)

British writer, perhaps best known for *The Prestige* (1995). Although he first appeared within the science-fiction genre magazines, his work goes beyond normal genre definitions. Many show his fascination with the transcendental relationship between people and their landscape. *A Dream of Wessex* (1977) follows an experiment where a group of people dream of a future Britain dominated by the Soviet Union with the exception of southern Britain, now separated from the mainland. Through their dreams they create a virtual world that becomes every bit as real as our own. In *The Affirmation* (1981), the narrator, Peter Sinclair, struggling to come to terms with his life, tries to bring order to his past and steadily creates an alternate existence. This imagined life increasingly takes hold until within that life Sinclair begins to write his autobiography, which is the start of *The Affirmation*, creating a loop like an ouroboros or even a Möbius strip. Like J.G. Ballard, Priest has been fascinated with time and impinging realities. His most extreme work is *The Inverted World* (1974), where time is measured in distance not duration, whilst both *The Extremes* (1998) and *The Separation* (2002) explore ambient time and overlapping worlds.

Cover of Christopher Priest's *The Affirmation* (1983).
X.958/28526

capable of dreams that change reality. He is manipulated by his psychiatrist who creates a device to influence Orr's dreams in the hope of a better world, but succeeds in only compounding the problems.

The ability to enter someone's dream and in some way influence it is fundamental to what would later develop as virtual reality. This idea first appeared in 'Dreams Are Sacred' (1948) by Peter Phillips. A fantasy author has succumbed to his own creations and is trapped in a coma. Doctors link his mind to another's who must enter the dream-world and defeat the creatures of the mind. John Brunner avoided the need for wires in

Telepathist (1964; US, *The Whole Man*), where a curative telepath enters people's minds to help treat them. In *The Dream Master* (1966) Roger Zelazny has a psychiatrist help cure patients through direct links to their imagination, but encounters a more powerful mind. With *Mindplayers* (1987), Pat Cadigan brought the concept into the cyberpunk era with her 'madcaps', which allow anyone to enter and explore the minds of others. Jeff Noon's *Vurt* (1993) uses the eponymous hallucinogenic drug to create a shared virtual reality, whilst the films *Dreamscape* (1984) and *Inception* (2010) take us into dream-worlds now almost indistinguishable from cyberspace.

Just imagine. You can control your dreams or influence others. Suppose you discovered that someone else has shared the same dream as you, at the same time. What would that mean?

The development of computer networks provided a believable scientific basis for the creation of dream-worlds within cyberspace.

The word 'cyberspace' first appeared in William Gibson's story 'Burning Chrome' (1982), later incorporated into his seminal cyberpunk novel *Neuromancer* (1984). It is derived from 'cybernetics', coined in 1947 by Norbert Wiener to define the connectivity between communication and feedback in any particular system. It easily lent itself to computer networks and the suffix '-space' added the concept of a world created by those networks, a world of 'consensual hallucination', as Gibson described it.

The phrase 'virtual reality', as we now use it, is attributed to computer-scientist Jaron Lanier who adopted it in about 1982 to refer to the environment developed with his headset and glove devices, which allowed a personal interface with a computer simulation. It also included the first 'avatars' or alter egos. The term itself, along with 'virtual matrix', had been used by Australian writer Damien Broderick in *The Judas Mandala*, which though not published until 1982 had been completed in 1975. The meaning here, though, related to a number of alternate futures and realities rather than a simulated world.

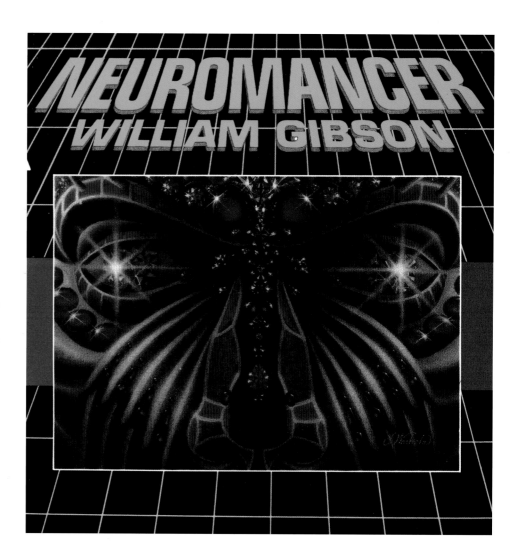

Above right Detail from the cover of *Neuromancer* by William Gibson (1984), the first edition of the book that launched cyberspace. Art by Richard Berry.

Far right *Science Wonder Stories*, May 1930, cover by Frank R. Paul for 'City of the Living Dead' by Laurence Manning and Fletcher Pratt.

William Gibson (born 1948)

American writer, best known for *Neuromancer* (1984) and regarded as one of the founding fathers of 'cyberpunk' – an outlook (rather than a movement) that portrays a highly urbanized, overpopulated and corrupt future society, dominated by the interfaces between sophisticated information networks, artificial intelligences (AIs) and nanotechnology. By plugging into the networks, individuals can interact with the virtual reality created by a shared illusion, which Gibson called 'cyberspace', in effect computer dream-worlds. Gibson's *Neuromancer*, though not the first story or book to develop this concept, defined it so completely as to become the definitive text. *Neuromancer* – the title is itself a play on 'new romancer' – also highlighted the increasing impotency of the individual against the corporate conglomerate, so that even Gibson's clever but corrupt protagonist seems heroic in his failed attempts to thwart big business. Gibson wrote two sequels, *Count Zero* (1986) and *Mona Lisa Overdrive* (1988), in which we see ever more transcendental AIs, imagery adopted with great effect in *The Matrix* film trilogy. In *Idoru* (1996) and *All Tomorrow's Parties* (1999) Gibson followed the effects of the cyber-revolution on global society and the human race itself.

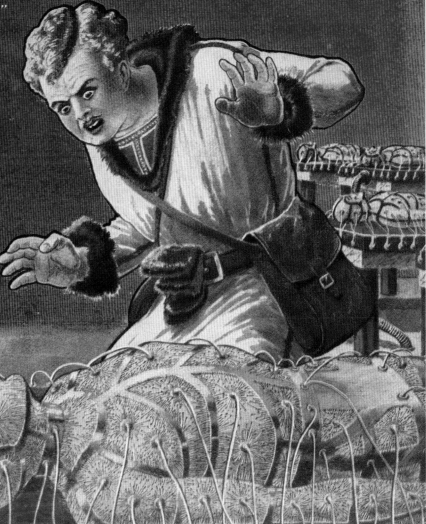

MYSTERY·ADVENTURE·ROMANCE

Science WONDER Stories

May

25 CENTS
Canada 30¢

A GERNSBACK PUBLICATION

HUGO GERNSBACK   Editor

"The City of the Living Dead"
by LAURENCE MANNING and
FLETCHER PRATT

other

Science Fiction Stories

by DR. DAVID H. KELLER

ED EARL REPP

JOHN SCOTT CAMPBELL

When Vernor Vinge created his concept of cyberspace in *True Names* (1981), he called it the 'Other Plane'. A group of technogeeks create false identities for themselves (which we now call avatars) and try to manipulate the Other Plane, but are challenged by a new adversary that turns out to be an advanced artificial intelligence.

The idea of a global information network long preceded the rise of the internet or computers. As far back as 1909, in the remarkably prescient 'The Machine Stops', E.M. Forster envisaged a future where most of humanity lives underground in individual cells and relies on 'the Machine' for all its needs and for global interaction. Forster shows the perils of overreliance on technology when, eventually, the machine stops. A similar vision of the decadence and fallibility of a machine-regulated society appeared in 'The City of the Living Dead' (1930) by Laurence Manning and Fletcher Pratt where a future world has reverted to a pre-industrial state but until recently an enclave survived of humans plugged in to dream machines, existing solely for their 'virtual' lives.

Aldous Huxley went some way to virtuality in *Brave New World* (1932) with his 'feelies', a cinema experience that added touch to sound and vision. Will F. Jenkins (better known under his alias Murray Leinster) predicted home computers and the internet in 'A Logic Named Joe' (1946). His network develops an intelligence of its own, the first hint of a computer reality. In Ray Bradbury's 'The Veldt' (1950), a home is installed with the latest technology including computer-simulated dreamscapes in the nursery that become all too real. In *Simulacron-3* (1964; aka *Counterfeit World*), filmed as *The Thirteenth Floor* (1999), Daniel F. Galouye has advertisers create a virtual city to enable them to undertake market research. Those who exist in this city are utterly unaware that they are computer simulations.

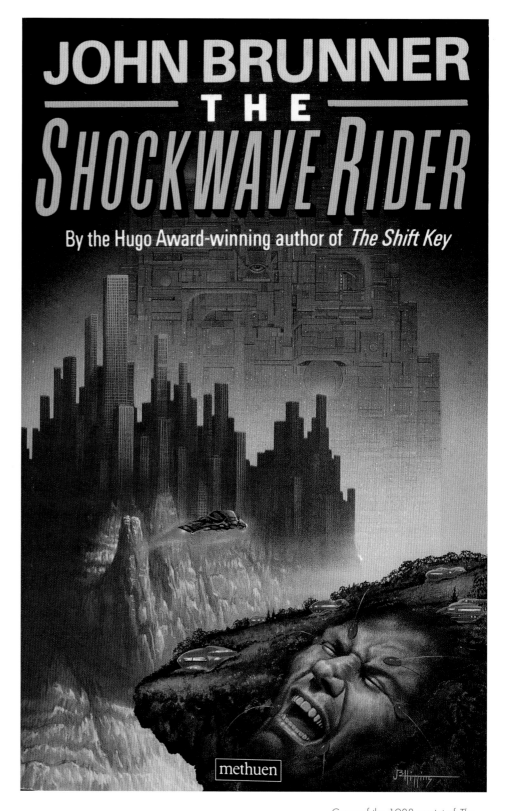

JOHN BRUNNER
THE
SHOCKWAVE RIDER

By the Hugo Award-winning author of *The Shift Key*

methuen

Cover of the 1988 reprint of *The Shockwave Rider* by John Brunner, illustrated by John Higgins. This is the book that created the 'computer worm'.

In his study of future technology, *Summa Technologiae* (1964), Stanislaw Lem foresaw the potential to override human perception with a simulated one. He called it 'phantomology'. Lem recognized the disorientation that this might cause, an issue that was central to his novel *Kongres Futurologiczny* (*The Futurological Congress*, 1971), where different realities are created by drugs rather than computer simulations.

In the 1950s science-fiction writers considered what might happen if people developed telepathic powers. If everybody were telepathic there would be no secrecy in the world and everyone would have access to everybody's thoughts – a kind of telepathic virtual reality. Alfred Bester wrote the definitive telepath novel in *The Demolished Man* (1953), which asked the question: how do you commit a murder in a world of no secrets? Part of the process included creating blocking devices, not unlike computer worms.

A decade before the emergence of the internet, John Brunner recognized the dangers of a global computer network in *The Shockwave Rider* (1975). Brunner developed his novel from Alvin Toffler's *Future Shock* (1970), which forecast the acceleration of technological progress to the point where people would be overwhelmed – he called it 'information overload'. Brunner envisaged a near future where government control via technology is all intrusive. His protagonist manages to hide himself from surveillance by manipulating the networks and creating false personas. He creates several computer 'worms' (the first use of the term) to retrieve data and disrupt the network.

Virtual reality has now become an accepted norm in computer games and animations, and the development and use of this technology continues to evolve

rapidly. Australian writer Greg Egan uses virtuality as a home for uploads of human personalities in *Permutation City* (1994). This provides a form of immortality except that the virtual humans find life tedious. Egan's *Permutation City* goes further and questions the nature of reality. This question goes to the heart of science and quantum mechanics. Theoretical physicists have suggested that the entire universe is a mathematical construct and that reality may be a hologram. In 'The World as a Hologram' (1994), Leonard Susskind proposed that reality is a three-dimensional projection of two-dimensional data stored in the universe's event horizon! Science fiction has yet to explore this in detail, though in *Permutation City* Egan developed similar thinking that the whole of reality could be a computer simulation, a form of 'cosmic anagram'.

In *Labirint otrazhenii* (*Labyrinth of Reflections*, 1997) by Sergey Lukyanenko, virtual reality can be accessed via a program that induces enhanced awareness in the user. It leads to the creation of a virtual city, Deeptown, which is explored in two sequels.

In *Air* (2005), Geoff Ryman switched everything around. A new information technology is created making everyone's minds part of an airborne internet that brings cyberspace directly into our heads. Indeed, our whole souls. This novel explores the impact that such a significant change – a global telepathic virtual world – brings to a small, isolated village in Asia that had been the last to be connected to the old-style internet. In a novel that blends past, present and future in a seamless tapestry, Ryman shows us that the virtual world is simply all of us, each one remaining unique, but contributing to a unifying whole.

Just imagine. You are involved in a computer-simulated game which does not react as you expect but introduces characters you do not know. Is this part of the game or has the simulation taken over?

Dream-worlds and Computer Worlds are essentially both worlds of the mind. But what of the world about us? Is our world real or an illusion or something other than how we perceive it?

This may seem a subject for metaphysics, but the question of what is reality is fundamental to science fiction which questions understanding, interpretation and perception. H. G. Wells touched on it in 'The Country of the Blind' (1904) where a traveller finds his way into an otherwise impenetrable valley where the inhabitants are blind with no concept of sight and no preparedness to understand. One could read this as a parable for humanity unable to understand what is around us. Science fiction writers like to withdraw those veils and show readers what the world may really be like.

One of the first to explore this was Charles Fort. He wrote no science fiction of his own, but collected a mass of data on unexplained phenomena – such as fish falling from the sky, spontaneous combustion or unidentified flying objects – which he published in several books from *The Book of the Damned* (1919) to *Wild Talents* (1932). Though Fort intended to present the data for others to analyze, he could not resist making some observations, of which his most famous was 'I think we're property'. He suggested that there might be alien creatures, perhaps living in the upper atmosphere, who guard us like cattle. Fort's books were highly influential, giving rise to a significant school of thought. One of the best known novels to emerge was *Sinister Barrier* (1939; book, 1948) by Eric Frank Russell, in which several scientists die in

Right Cover of September 1951 *Galaxy* featuring Robert A. Heinlein's *The Puppet Masters*, illustrated by Don Sibley.

Philip K. Dick (1928–82)

American writer who since his death has developed a significant cult following. Several of his books have been filmed, notably as *Blade Runner* (1982), *Total Recall* (1990) and *Minority Report* (2002). Dick's plots draw heavily upon paranoia and delusion. In *Time Out of Joint* (1959), a man who is good at predicting becomes worried by various odd events, some of which feel familiar. Only gradually does he realize he is being kept in a fabricated environment and his predictive powers are being used to track impending targets in a war between Earth and the lunar colony. One of Dick's most unsettling books is *Ubik* (1969), which is set in a near future where psi-powers are rampant and anti-telepaths are employed to block mind reading. It is also possible to be preserved after death in a half-life, with the aid of a product called Ubik. When several individuals find the world becoming increasingly surreal the question is whether they are alive or dead.

Questions of reality pervade most of Dick's books. Survivors of a nuclear accident experience surreal events in *Eye in the Sky* (1957) because half of them are living in the dream-worlds of the other half. In *A Maze of Death* (1970) misfits moved to a strange planet discover they are the subjects of an experiment that they themselves are conducting. In *A Scanner Darkly* (1977) the protagonist has a dual personality – half narcotics agent, half drug dealer – and so pursues himself. *The Three Stigmata of Palmer Eldritch* (1965) is perhaps Dick's most transcendental novel, and impossible to summarize because it involves various hallucinogenic worlds, false or changed personalities, bluff and counter-bluff, all interwoven to extinguish any understanding of reality.

Brian Lewis's cover illustration for the serialization of Philip K. Dick's *Time Out of Joint* in *New Worlds*, January 1960.
P.P.6018.thx

NEW WORLDS
SCIENCE FICTION

No. 90
VOLUME 30
2/6

O'MARA'S ORPHAN
James White

UNDER AN
ENGLISH HEAVEN
Brian W. Aldiss

MUMBO-JUMBO MAN
Philip E. High

Serial
TIME OUT OF JOINT
Part Two
Philip K. Dick

Features

14th Year
of Publication

Galaxy

SCIENCE FICTION

SEPTEMBER 1951

35¢

ANC

THE PUPPET MASTERS
by Robert A. Heinlein

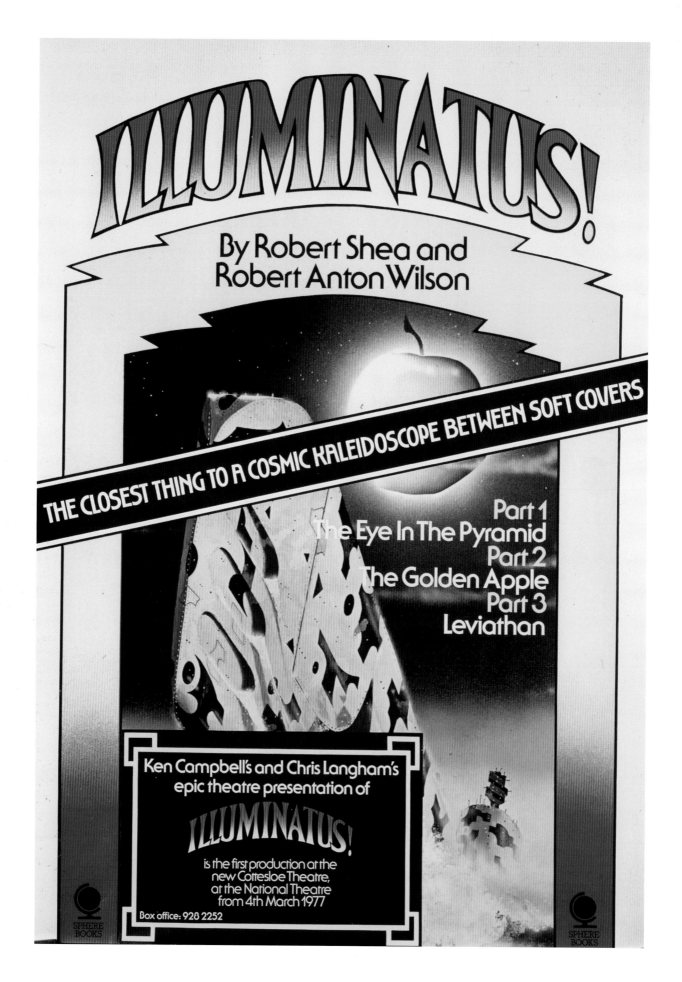

Above First British edition of *Ægypt* by John Crowley (1988). Cover by John Avon. YC.1988.a.9978

Left Poster for the National Theatre's production of *Illuminatus!* directed by Ken Campbell in 1977.

unusual circumstances, and it requires an undercover investigation to unravel the truth they had discovered about aliens in our midst.

The idea that there could be aliens amongst us, somehow blending in to society, was first popularized by John W. Campbell, Jr in 'Who Goes There?' (1938), where a shape-changing alien infiltrates a base in the Antarctic and takes on the form of any of the men there. The film version, *The Thing From Another World* (1951), is remembered for its final warning, 'Keep Watching the Skies', which became as well known a paranoid warning as the McCarthyist 'Reds Under the Beds'.

Robert A. Heinlein's *The Puppet Masters* (1951; complete version, 1990) took full advantage of the paranoia of the McCarthy era in the United States by paralleling the fear of Communism with the idea that small slug-like aliens have attached themselves to humans and taken control. This was the period when flying-saucer sightings were on the increase, following the UFO sightings by Kenneth Arnold and the alleged alien crash-landing at Roswell in June 1947. Jack Finney built on this fear with *The Body Snatchers* (1954), where alien spores develop into pods in which grow replica humans.

The idea that someone might believe they live in a fantasy world was the subject of a psychiatrist's study, 'The Jet-Propelled Couch' by Robert Lindner (in *The Fifty-Minute Hour*, 1955). One of his patients, whom he called Kirk, had experienced an oppressive childhood and had retreated into the world of space opera imagined from the pulp magazines where he was the ruler of the planet Seraneb. His imagination had created a complete life which, to Kirk, was more real than his Earth-bound one. It has long been believed, though not confirmed, that the individual called Kirk was the American political scientist Paul M. Linebarger who wrote science fiction as Cordwainer Smith.

Smith's early story 'Scanners Live in Vain' (1950), dealt with sensory-deprived humans who serve as barriers to help normal humans survive the trauma of space travel. Once in a while scanners are allowed to return to the real world when their senses are reconnected.

In the film *The Truman Show* (1998), based on a script by Andrew Niccol, the entire life of Truman Burbank has been filmed for the last thirty years, round the clock, but he is unaware of it, and has no idea that he is living on a film set. It is only when a number of things go wrong that Truman begins to question his life. Niccol reversed the idea for *S1m0ne* (2002), where he creates a computer-simulated woman for a film whom he then passes off as real.

The complexity of understanding the reality of the present is even more exacerbated if we believe the past is also a fabrication – that beneath the thin veneer of recorded history are those secret histories of what really happened. The major work was the original Illuminatus! Trilogy – *The Eye in the Pyramid*, *The Golden Apple* and *Leviathan* (all 1975) – by Robert Anton Wilson and Robert J. Shea, plus various sequels by either partner. The series engenders a belief in conspirators who have shaped history and events to their own ends to ultimately control the Earth.

Several of the books by Neal Stephenson deal with data manipulation and redefining history, notably *Cryptonomicon* (1999) and his Baroque Cycle, *Quicksilver* (2003), *The Confusion* and *The System of the World* (both 2004). In a similar vein is John Crowley's Ægypt sequence, *The Solitudes* (1987 as Ægypt), *Love & Sleep* (1994), *Dæmonomania* (2000) and *Endless Things* (2007), which in a multi-strand, orthogonal approach gradually reveals the hidden layers of history. These books treat hermeticism and alchemical studies as a background to understanding the true nature of the world.

Just imagine. You peel back the curtains in the morning and for a moment see something that is not part of this world, and then normal service is resumed. Has the real world for a split second revealed itself? What would you do?

Future Worlds

Science fiction has the whole span of time with which to play, but the vast majority takes place in the future – so much so that the future is synonymous with science fiction. Hence, it is perhaps surprising that the idea of stories set in the future came late to fiction, and their appearance is a key part of the development of science fiction as a field in its own right.

It is true that throughout history there have been seers, oracles and prophets who claim to foresee the future, whether predicting the outcome of a battle or witnessing apocalyptic visions of the Earth's last days. Religion aside, some 'prophets' are still quoted today, notably Michel de Nostredame, or Nostradamus, whose *Les Propheties* (*The Prophecies*, 1555) has been cited to predict almost anything in any age.

Science fiction, though, is not a vehicle for prediction. There have been occasional good 'hits', some of which will be explored in this section, but generally science fiction has a poor record of accurately forecasting anything. What science fiction does is extrapolate change from a given point and suggest possible futures. That forecast may of itself prove influential and bring about change to try and avoid that very prediction. The future warning story, particularly as regards the possibility of war or invasion or, more recently, ecological change, is a powerful tool and has proved popular.

Most memorably, science fiction creates images or ideas that suggest the future and may inspire scientists to pursue those goals. These include both technological and social change and are most potent in the imagery of future cities, homes, transport and daily life on the positive side, or warfare, overpopulation, disease and social decline on the negative side. Other images, such as automation – robots are a common image of the future – and genetic engineering, may be seen as either good or bad with opinions divided over their benefits.

It is this concept of change, particularly technological change, for good or for ill, and how humanity might adapt to its challenges that is key to science fiction and which is explored in this section.

Right The city of Metropolis from the film
Metropolis (1927), directed by Fritz Lang. The
original designs for the city were by Otto Hunte.

Imagining the Future

For most people throughout history the thought of 'change' meant the weather, harvest and growing old. There was the occasional new monarch and there were wars, but this was all part of the cycle of life and no one gave much thought to whether it would ever change.

Early attempts are thus rare and isolated. The pamphlet *Aulicus his dream of the King's sudden coming to London* (1644) by Parliamentarian minister Francis Cheynell was a piece of political propaganda, portraying what might happen if Charles I regained power. Michel de Pure's incomplete *Epigone, histoire du siècle futur* (Epigone, History of the Next Century, 1659) is really a traveller's tale set in an undefined future.

It was not until well into the eighteenth century that writers cast their imagination into the future. This was a sign of literary freedom emerging in the Age of Enlightenment, as well as a recognition that the world was changing, at least politically if not technologically.

In *Memoirs of the Twentieth Century* (1733), the Irish writer Samuel Madden gave an account of the descendants of the Jacobite Comte de Gablis in the highly Protestant world of George VI. Madden only completed the first volume (of six planned) and, on the day of publication, he destroyed 900 of the 1000-copy print run. Yet the book lived on. The anonymous *The Reign of George VI* (1763), evidently influenced by Madden's work, shows Russia in the ascendancy and the outbreak of a war that engulfs most of Europe between the years 1900 and 1922 but ends in a British victory. That prospect is reversed in the anonymous *Private Letters from an American in England to His Friends in America* (1769), set thirty years in the future. It depicts a Britain so degenerate, thanks to over-indulgence, profligate lawyers, the Scots and idle bishops, that it has ceded its government to America.

None of these books made any serious attempt to envisage scientific progress. It fell to the French playwright Louis-Sébastien Mercier to portray a transformed future in *L'An deux mille quatre cent quarante* (The Year 2440, 1771), which depicts a new, enlightened France. It was the first utopian novel to be set in the future, albeit presented as a dream. Here at last was a book that projected political, social and some scientific change (particularly in medicine) throughout Europe, Asia and Africa. Mercier developed the ideas of Jean-Jacques Rousseau and the Enlightenment with significant revisions to religion (Catholicism has been replaced by a new form of Deism), social class (future kings are raised amongst the poor), education (progressive, with all past teachings and literature destroyed) and the law (lawyers are almost nonexistent).

The book was condemned by the Inquisition and had to be published in the Netherlands, but still went through many

Right 'The Century of Invention'. A cartoon by Charles Jameson Grant published in 1834, depicting the Century of Invention to the year 2000, an era of perpetual motion where steam carriages and airships have made the horse an endangered species.

Below *Le Monde tel qu'il sera* by Émile Souvestre (1846). Illustration from the Portuguese edition, Lisbon, 1859.
12515.i.3

editions, revisions and translations and was the first utopia to be published in North America in 1795. Mercier did not admit his authorship until the 1791 edition, to which he added a preface where he hinted that the book may have encouraged (with other writings) the French Revolution of 1789. Mercier was actively involved in the Revolution, although he was imprisoned during the Reign of Terror.

The wide translation of Mercier's book spread his ideas to other countries. In Scandinavia, *Anno 7603* (The Year 7603, 1781), a comic play by the Danish-Norwegian poet, Johan Wessel, has a couple transported to a distant future where the gender roles are reversed and women are dominant. In Germany, *Ini: ein Roman aus dem ein und zwanzigstein Jahrhundert* (Ini: a Novel of the Twenty-First Century, 1810), a romance by the Prussian Julius von Voss, depicts a united Europe, with its capital at Rome. There have been many improvements in social conditions and education, and such scientific advances as streamlined balloons pulled by eagles, floating islands pulled by whales, artificial organs and perpetual motion.

Mercier's compatriot Rétif de la Bretonne was the first to create a future history, charting a chronology of events

into the far future. His two-volume *Les Posthumes* (1802) includes a series of accounts by Lord Multipliandre who has found a way of spiritual travel occupying different bodies far into the future. No dates are given but millenia pass. A comet becomes the Earth's second moon, which leads to floods and other catastrophes. The continents change. Humans, animals and plants evolve (though not by Darwinian principles), including the appearance of long-lived winged humans.

In Russia, some writers saw the potential of future fiction to promote advances for their country. The journalist and publisher, Faddei Bulgarin, described a reborn Siberia in *Pravdopodobnye nebylitsy, ili stranstvovanie po svetu v dvadsat' deviatom veke* (Plausible Fantasies or a Journey in the 29th Century, 1824). The narrator's body is preserved into the future and reawakens when climate change has turned Siberia into a paradise garden. There is an Eskimo empire as well as the Russian, though Arabic is the language of culture. New technologies extract fuel from the atmosphere and grow food in underwater gardens, and there are new drugs that enhance the senses.

In his unfinished *4338-i god* (The Year 4338, begun 1835), fellow Russian

Prince Vladimir Odoevsky depicts a future where Russia is a highly technologically advanced power. Most other nations have not survived and people have reverted to barbarism, except China. Though also culturally advanced, it remains technologically undeveloped and hopes to learn from Russia. The story takes the form of a series of letters written by a young Chinese student visiting Russia. A class system remains in Russia and although the lower classes have access to education, they do not understand its significance and so are not accepted by enlightened scientists, scholars and artists. Many technological advances are mentioned and include the equivalent of air traffic, synthetic materials, electronic stimulants and telephones.

In Britain, there was concern over the consequences of political or social reform. There was a growing belief in what became called the March of Intellect, a phrase describing the thirst for knowledge and scientific research that came in the wake of the industrial revolution. Philanthropists such as Robert Owen used it as a rallying cry for social reform, whilst no less than Queen Caroline (the estranged wife of George IV) saw it as the growth of true democracy. But the sceptical British were not all sure where it would lead. The caricaturist William Heath produced a series of prints on the March of Intellect showing such possibilities as a vacuum tube transportation system and bridges across the English Channel and Straits of Gibraltar.

Thoughts on the March of Intellect encouraged Jane Webb, later to become better known as horticulturalist Jane Loudon, to pen *The Mummy* (1827). Written in her late teens, the novel takes the crude idea (based on Mary Shelley's *Frankenstein*) that an Egyptian mummy is revived and is able to use its superior knowledge to help the British monarchy. But behind the gothic plot is a rationalization of how society in the year 2126 had developed over three centuries. The populace has taken advantage of increased education and knowledge, but this has led to them becoming amoral and rebellious. Both the United States and Spain have become tyrannical republics. Britain has reverted to Catholicism and is ruled by an absolute matriarchal monarch. Webb refers to many technological advances including long-distance airships, automaton judges, weather control and steam-powered houses.

Other writers used future fiction to highlight concerns over progress. In *The Last Peer* (1851, published anonymously), set in 1901, Britain has lost its empire and is in decline. Landowners have become dispossessed because the rise of machinery has removed the need for cultivation. Likewise, in *2000 Years Hence* (1868) by Henry O'Neil, Britain's power has significantly reduced and is now governed by New Zealand. The country's decline was due to the Reform Acts of 1832 and 1867,

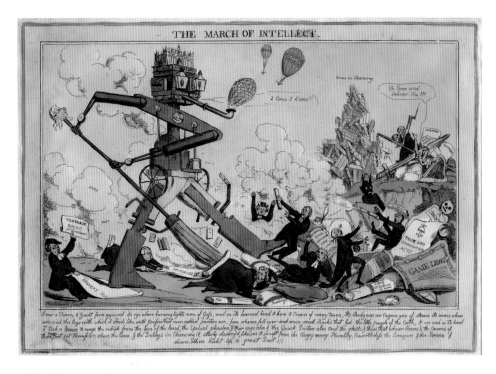

The March of Intellect. A series of posters produced by William Heath (under the alias Paul Pry) between 1825 and 1829 depicting how the thirst for education and scientific discovery is changing the world though not necessarily for the better.

which gave too much power to the general populace.

The French novelist Émile Souvestre did not see a rosy future either. The son of a civil engineer, he was well equipped to conjecture technological progress in *Le Monde tel qu'il sera* (The World as it Will Be, 1846), set in the year 3000. He foresaw writing machines, telephones, submarines, state-controlled parenting and eugenics within an increasingly corrupt society. Souvestre saw this as the result of capitalism and commercialism leading to the inevitable slavery to the machine and the markets. The novel of the future had reached a crossroads where it could forecast either prosperity and salvation or over-mechanization and servitude.

In May 1871 the venerable Scottish *Blackwood's Magazine* published 'The Battle of Dorking', which told of the successful invasion of Britain by German forces. The peace treaty leads to the dismantling of the British Empire and the crushing of British industry. The author, Lieutenant-Colonel George Tomkyns Chesney, was a long-serving army officer who had concerns over Britain's preparedness to counter an invasion.

The story appeared at the end of the Franco-Prussian War, where the combined German and Prussian forces had demonstrated not only their military superiority but also their adaptability, through the use of railways and anti-balloon artillery. It caused an outcry, and the Prime Minister, William Gladstone, was obliged to calm public concern against the 'alarmism' the story had created.

'The Battle of Dorking' was not the first story to propose an invasion of Britain. During the Napoleonic Wars there had been various items penned by both sides, such as the anonymous *The Invasion; or, What Might Have Been* (1798) countered by the French drama *La Descente en Angleterre* (The Raid on England, 1798). It happened again when Napoleon III took power, with the anonymous pamphlet *History of the sudden and terrible invasion of England by the French* (1851), but none of these had the impact of 'The Battle of Dorking'. Chesney's story was convincing and highlighted the proven German military might. There was a host of anonymous sequels, starting with *The Siege of London* (1871), which stretched on for years including *The Invasion of England* (1882), and *The Battle of Worthing* (1887).

In France, the multi-talented Albert Robida wrote and illustrated *La Guerre au vingtième siècle* (War in the Twentieth Century, 1887), following the experiences of a soldier and airman in a worldwide war that began in 1945. Robida depicts aerial bombardment, submarine battles, huge bunker-like tanks and chemical warfare. In America, modern technology was at the fore in *The Great War Syndicate* (1889)

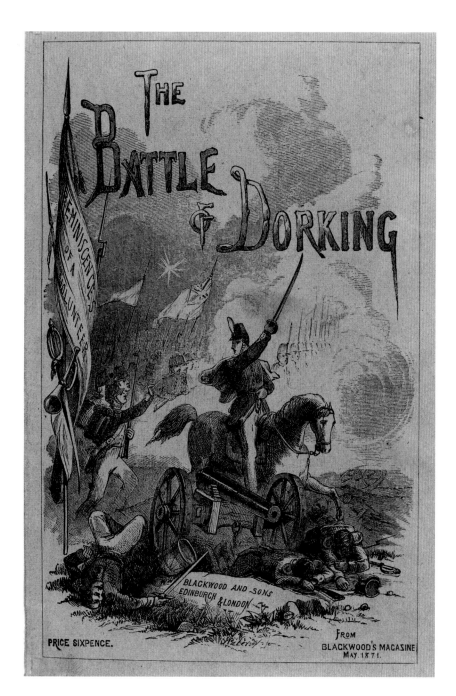

by Frank R. Stockton, where a group of industrialists fight a war on behalf of the American government and defeat Britain. Their weapons include rocket-powered bombs and mini-submarines that sabotage shipping. But whereas other countries produced future war fiction concentrating on the conflict, the British were uniquely paranoid about invasion and being ill-prepared.

A new approach to warning the authorities came with *The Great War of 189–* (1892), produced by a bevy of high-ranking naval and military men including

Left *The Battle of Dorking* by George Chesney, one of the most influential of all future war stories.
C.193.B.18(2)

Right Advertisement in *The Times* for the serialization of *The Invasion of 1910* by William Le Queux in the *Daily Mail*, showing a map of the conflict.

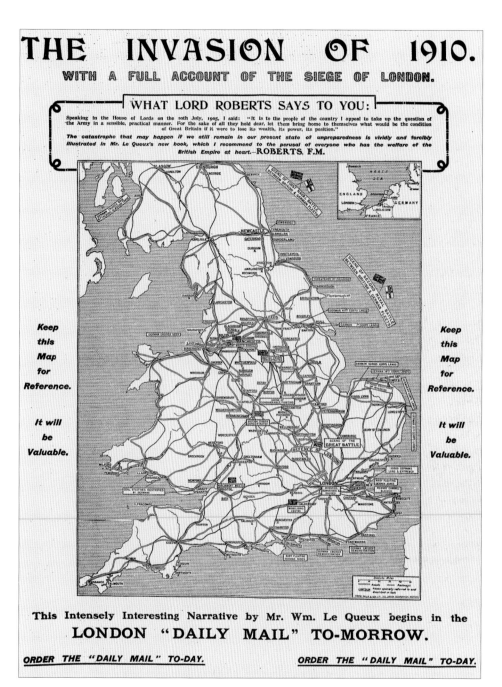

Above *The Great War in England in 1897* (1894) by William Le Queux.
012630.L.1

Rear-Admiral Philip Colomb, Colonel John Maurice and Captain Frederick Maude. It was compiled as a series of dispatches from war correspondents giving an immediacy and verisimilitude to the story. The early parts bear a striking similarity to the real events that led up to World War I, starting with the assassination of European royalty by Serbian anarchists. A chain of treaties leads inevitably to British involvement in a European war, except that in this story Britain is an ally of Germany against the Russians and French.

In *The Final War* (1896), set in 1898, Louis Tracy describes an all-out World War that begins when Germany and France join forces (with Russian support) to invade Britain. The allies are defeated, and America intervenes to overcome the Russians. Tracy's occasional collaborator, M.P. Shiel, outdid Tracy with *The Yellow Danger* (1898), where the Chinese take advantage of a complex war in Europe to try and conquer the world with an army of 180 million, but are defeated by germ warfare.

Amongst the many writers who contributed to this genre, two came to dominate the field: George Griffith and William Le Queux. George Griffith's fiction was the most technological, much in the vein of Jules Verne's work, though Le Queux's had the most impact.

William Le Queux was a journalist and early radio pioneer who became better known for his spy stories. In *The Great War in England in 1897* (1894), he adopted Colomb's reportage approach. It describes a war between Britain and Russia, with Germany as Britain's ally. Despite British naval supremacy the Russians invade Scotland and lay waste to cities as they advance south, but they are eventually defeated south of London (near Dorking!).

Le Queux repeated the format with *The Invasion of 1910* (1906), which was serialized in the *Daily Mail*, complete with maps, documents and newspaper reports. The story charts the invasion of Britain by German forces with Britain, as usual, unprepared. Many British cities are destroyed, but resistance in the south, under the League of Defenders, fights back and is victorious. The Prime Minister called Le Queux's work 'alarmist', which led to a heated exchange between the two men – all of which helped the book to become a huge bestseller.

Throughout this same period German future war fiction had been certain about the defeat of Britain. Britain is humiliated in *Der Weltkrieg – Deutsche Träume* (World War – German Dreams, 1904; translated as *The Coming Conquest of England*) by August

The Swoop by P.G. Wodehouse (1909). The popularity of the future war story was such that it was lampooned by no less than Wodehouse, who has Britain invaded simultaneously by nine different nations (including Monaco). The victors are ultimately defeated by the Boy Scouts.
012331.g.24

" He had never been north of the Midland counties, and the multitude of factories and chimneys—the latter for the most part obsolete and smokeless now, superseded by huge electric generating stations that consumed their own reek—old railway viaducts, mono-rail networks and goods yards, and the vast areas of dingy homes and narrow streets, spreading aimlessly,—struck him as though Camberwell and Rotherhithe had run to seed."

H.G. Wells's *War in the Air* serialized in *Pall Mall Magazine* during 1908. Illustration by A.C. Michael.

P.P.6004.gln

Niemann. The English translator called the book a 'day-dream'. The sub-title to Rudolf Martin's *Berlin-Bagdad: Das Deutsche Weltreich im Zeitalter der Luftschiffahrt, 1910–1931* (Berlin-Bagdad: The German World-Empire in the Age of Airship Travel, 1910–1931, 1907) shows how positive they were of their control of the air.

Martin's book almost certainly encouraged Wells to write *The War in the Air* (1908). Wells had already shown how Britain had succumbed to a Martian invasion in *The War of the Worlds* (1898), but in *The War in the Air* he wrote his most potent warning story. He describes how all the major nations develop heavier-than-air craft leading to a World War that destroys civilization. Wells believed that the aeroplane was the most important invention of the last sixty years.

Of course, none of these warning stories did anything to avert World War I, which in its scale and cost of lives was far greater than anything envisaged, except by Wells. On the eve of the war, Arthur Conan Doyle wrote a short story, 'Danger!' (1914), which showed how Britain could be defeated by a submarine blockade. British authorities ignored Doyle's warnings, but the Germans didn't. Senior German officials, including Admiral von Capelle, later claimed they got their idea for blockading Britain from Doyle's story.

A contrast to the gloom of the future war story was the growing number of stories considering the benefits of scientific progress. The future Poet Laureate, Alfred Lord Tennyson, had included a vision of the future in his poem 'Locksley Hall' (1842), where a soldier, pausing at his childhood home, reflects on his life and considers the future. Though he sees the heavens 'fill with commerce' and the nation's 'airy navies grappling' he also looks on to 'the Parliament of Man, the Federation of the World'.

Félix Bodin had also been positive about future prospects in *Le Roman de l'avenir* (The Novel of the Future, 1834). Though his technological predictions were limited by the science of the day, he held cautious hopes for a steady if chequered route to world peace. Jules Verne, on the other hand, was pessimistic. His second novel, *Paris au XXᵉ siècle* (Paris in the 20th Century, written: 1863; published: 1994) was rejected by his publisher as too gloomy. In Verne's future, technology and commercialism have superseded art and literature and stifled creativity – although the perfection of weapons has led to a military stalemate. Verne is often seen as a writer about the future, but most of

his stories are set in the present though may contain futuristic style inventions, such as the submarine and the propeller-driven airship. Almost all of his creations were projections of existing machines. Yet Verne's reputation overshadowed those of his countrymen, some of whom, like the remarkable visionary Albert Robida, created a wealth of futuristic images.

The wonders of science had been one of the reasons behind the Great Exhibition held in London in 1851 and again at the Exposition Universelle in Paris in 1889 (for which the Eiffel Tower was built) and the World's Fair in Chicago in

Albert Robida (1848–1926)

French artist and novelist who earned a reputation as a caricaturist. Moving from illustration to text, Robida wrote a parody of Jules Verne's novels with *Voyages très extraordinaire de Saturnin Farandoul* (*The Extraordinary Voyages of Saturnin Farandoul*, 1879) in which Farandoul is raised by apes on a remote island and becomes a pre-Tarzanesque adventurer. Robida's next book, which was copiously illustrated, was *Le Vingtième siècle* (*The Twentieth Century*, 1883). The slight plot, about a woman's search for work in 1952, allows Robida to explore the institutions of the next century alongside such inventions as the 'téléphonoscope' (or television), personal airships, a Transatlantic tunnel (or tube) and submarine cities. In addition to these inventions, in *La Vie électrique* (*The Electric Life*, 1890), Robida foresaw the transformation of the Sahara, overpopulation and gas warfare. Other horrors of war were portrayed in *La Guerre au vingtième siècle* (War in the Twentieth Century, 1887). When Robida witnessed the real thing he wrote a bleak depiction of the ultimate doomsday weapon in *L'Ingénieur Von Satanas* (Satanas the Engineer, 1919).

Left 'Guesses at Futurity' by Fred T. Jane from *Pall Mall Magazine*, 1894, showing home life and street lighting in the year 2000.
PP.6004.gln

Above left The cover from Albert Robida's 1890 volume, *La Vie électrique*.
12350.m.27

Above A scene from *La Vingtième siècle* (1883) showing the aero-taxi working through 'Un quartier embrouille' – the scrambled neighbourhood.
12350.m.15

1893. As the century reached its close, Victorian determination, French creativity and American entrepreneurship looked towards a scientifically transformed future. This was fuelled by the remarkable number of inventions pouring from a host of inventors, especially Thomas Edison at his research laboratory in Menlo Park, New Jersey, established in 1876. Edison is sometimes attributed with inventions that were not his own, but he often improved the inventions of others, such as the telephone and the light bulb, and gave the world the phonograph, street lighting and the 'movie'. Edison's rivalry with his former employee, Nikola Tesla, is the stuff of legend, and that relationship spurred on further research.

Edison's fame was such that he not only inspired much science fiction but also featured as a character. He takes a central role as the creator of an android woman in *L'Eve Future* (The Future Eve, 1886) by Villiers de l'Isle Adam. In *Recollections of the Late War with Canada* (1889) by Frank Rollins, Edison saves the day through his invention of electric torpedoes. In *Edison's Conquest of Mars* (1898; book, 1947), a follow-on to H.G. Wells's *War of the Worlds*, Garrett P. Serviss has the inventor create a disintegrator weapon and lead a fleet of spaceships to Mars to deter the Martians from another invasion.

Both Edison and Tesla appear in Cleveland Moffett's *The Conquest of America* (1916), when both seek to invent weapons to defeat the Germans who have taken control of New England in 1921. Edison is captured but rescued and eventually defeats the Germans.

The American novelist George Parsons Lathrop's novella, 'In the Deep of Time' (1897) is filled with ideas that had arisen from an interview with Edison. These included suspended animation, synthetic materials, anti-gravity, automated factories operated from one keyboard and books transmitted by telephone.

The 1880s onwards marked the era of invention and science fiction

"A MAN WITH A GHASTLY SCARLET HEAD FOLLOWS, SHOUTING THAT HE MUST GO BACK AND BUILD UP HIS RAY."

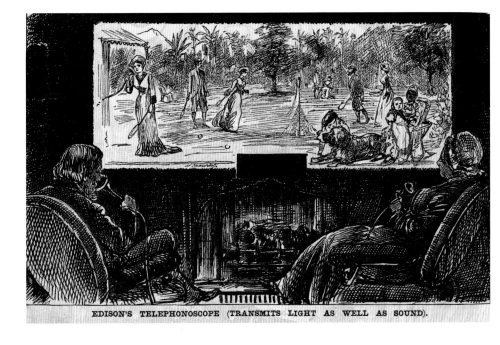

EDISON'S TELEPHONOSCOPE (TRANSMITS LIGHT AS WELL AS SOUND).

Left Rudyard Kipling's *With the Night Mail* (1909), illustrated by Frank Leyendecker. The story, first published in 1905, recounts problems encountered one night for the dirigibles that deliver mail across the Atlantic in the year 2000.
File 242

Right George du Maurier's cartoon in *Punch Almanack* for 1879 depicting the telephonoscope in the style of Albert Robida. Although this looks like a television it also seems to operate over the phone linked to a camera as in today's video telephones.
P.P.5276(3)

Super-calculator.

The super-calculator as forecast by I.O. Evans in *World of Tomorrow* in 1933.
20017.b.28

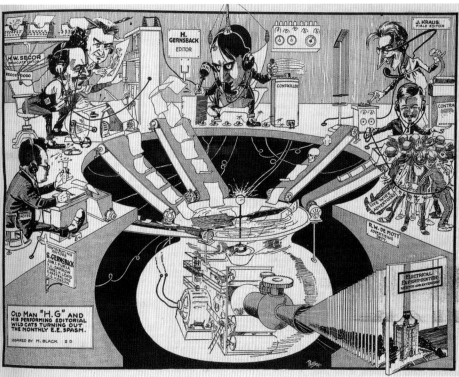

Frank R. Paul's sketch of Hugo Gernsback and the rest of the editorial staff of *The Electrical Experimenter*, April 1920.
A161 NPL

Just imagine. What new invention do you believe is needed that will change the world forever? And what will be its consequences – both for good and for ill?

Nikola Tesla portrayed by Warwick Goble in an interview published in *Pearson's Magazine*, May 1899. Tesla was called 'The New Wizard of the West'.
P.P.6004.gmq

responded. This was the real basis of science fiction, conjecturing on the possibilities of science. From here on, most popular magazines featured stories or pictures of unusual inventions. We have already seen that Albert Robida included a television in *Le Vingtième siècle* in 1883, the year before the German Paul Nipkow patented the idea of a rotating disk system. Five years earlier, the British cartoonist George du Maurier had depicted a telephonoscope or 'electric camera obscura' in the *Punch Almanack* issued in December 1878. To give it verisimilitude, Edison's name is attached to it.

Other predictions in fiction at this time include close-circuit television, invented in 1942 but first described in *The Great Awakening* (1899) by Albert Adams Merrill; an exoskeleton capable of lifting great weights, now called waldoes after Robert A. Heinlein's story

'Waldo' (1942), but described long before in Simon Newcomb's *His Wisdom the Defender* (1900); and a video-recorder, not invented until 1956, but described by L. Frank Baum in *The Master Key* (1901). A form of pre-paid debit card, not available until the 1980s, is used in *A Thousand Years Hence* (1903) by Ira S. Bunker, whilst the mobile phone, invented in 1973 but not commercially available until 1983, was described in an unaccredited story, 'A Glimpse into the Future' in the October 1909 issue of *Popular Electricity*.

Fred T. Jane, who compiled the first *Jane's Fighting Ships* in 1898, was better known as an artist and he produced a series of illustrations for *Pall Mall Magazine* during 1894–5 called 'Guesses at Futurity'. This showed eight scenes from the world of 2000, when various historical fashions have become the rage, homes are full of mod-cons, there is interplanetary

communication, mining on the Moon, synthetic food and rooftop gardens. Also set in the year 2000 is *The Crack of Doom* (1895) by Robert Cromie, the first book to explore the release of atomic energy from matter. Cromie did not go so far as to describe an atomic bomb, but the devastation caused when the energy is released destroys an island in the Pacific – not too dissimilar to what happened to Bikini Atoll with the nuclear tests of 1946.

The influence of Edison and Tesla went beyond inspiring invention stories. Hugo Gernsback, an immigrant from Luxembourg, had settled in the United States in 1904 and set up an importing company for electrical equipment chiefly for the burgeoning radio industry. Gernsback had invented his own portable radio in 1905. He issued a catalogue which he converted into the magazine *Modern Electrics* in 1908. He was a huge admirer of Edison, Tesla and other inventors, notably the radio pioneer Lee De Forest. Gernsback believed that the American nation, particularly its youth, should be encouraged to become experimenters and inventors and aspire to the achievements of his heroes. He thus directed *Modern Electrics* to the hobbyist and to stimulate their imagination he created a story, *Ralph 124C 41+* (1911–12; book, 1923). Ralph is a mastermind inventor in the year 2660. In the first episode he is talking to a girl in Switzerland via the 'telephot' when he realizes she is endangered by an avalanche, and he directs electrical forces to melt the snow. A romance ensues and when the girl is kidnapped by a Martian, Ralph tracks the spaceship by radar. Gernsback described the principles of radar over twenty years before Robert Watson-Watt developed it in Britain.

The story in *Ralph 124C 41+* is weak, but it was intended to promote a catalogue of inventions and inspire his

Left Frank R. Paul depicts genius inventor Ralph talking via the telephot to Alice in Switzerland from *Ralph 124C 41+*, first serialized in 1911–12. Taken from the Bison Books edition, 2000.

Right *Amazing Stories*, February 1928. The world's first science-fiction magazine. Cover by Frank R. Paul illustrating a scene from Hugo Gernsback's serial 'Baron Münchausen's Scientific Adventures'.
P.P.6383.ccs

readers. Gernsback encouraged story contributions to his magazine and its successor, *The Electrical Experimenter*, which was renamed *Science and Invention* in 1920. He called these stories scientific fiction, which he contracted to 'scientifiction', and in 1926 he began the first all 'scientifiction' magazine in the world, called *Amazing Stories*. Unaware of the earlier use of the phrase 'science fiction' by William Wilson, Gernsback coined the phrase himself in 1929 when he began a new magazine, *Science Wonder Stories*.

The success of Gernsback's magazines alerted other publishers and the 1930s saw a host of new titles. Chief amongst them was *Astounding Stories*, first issue January 1930, which from 1938, under new editor John W. Campbell, Jr, became the leading science-fiction magazine. It is still going today, as *Analog*. *Astounding Stories* was published as a pulp magazine. Before

long, Gernsback's magazines followed suit and the 1930s and 1940s was the era of the science-fiction pulps. Most of the leading science-fiction writers of the day debuted in these pulps, including Isaac Asimov, Robert A. Heinlein, Frederik Pohl, James Blish, A.E. van Vogt, Theodore Sturgeon, Henry Kuttner and C.L. Moore.

Gernsback was not the only publisher promoting science through fiction. His approach was echoed elsewhere. In Russia, Petr Soikin, prompted by science popularizer Iakov Perel'man, issued Mir Prikliuchenii (World of Adventures) starting in 1910 as a supplement to the leading science magazine. It ran mostly translated science fiction, but included commentary by Perel'man highlighting the scientific significance of stories. Perel'man has been called second only to Tsiolkovski in stimulating Russian interest in science.

In Sweden, mining engineer Otto

Witt turned to writing science fiction and detective stories for adolescents. From 1916 to 1920 he published *Hugin*, a magazine similar to *The Electrical Experimenter*, promoting science alongside fiction. In China the magazine *Kexue shijie* (Scientific World) ran from February 1903 to November 1904 with a special section for translations of science fiction, but it was not until 1939 that Gu Junzheng, China's Gernsback, issued *Kexue quwei* (Scientific Taste) to publish new science fiction alongside science features. These and many other magazines sought to encourage youngsters to become interested in science and technology and thereby help invent the future.

Cities of the Future

If any image came to symbolize the future it was that of the city, though it is an image of contrasts. On the one hand, a city of towering skyscrapers, moving walkways, electric lighting and personal aircars represents progress and achievement, but overcrowded cities of disease, filth and decadence represent mankind and ecology out of control, leading to death and ruin.

This dichotomy was evident from the start, showing a love-hate or hope-fear relationship with the city, which had sucked in people during the nineteenth century at the cost of the rural society. The growing number of skyscrapers from the 1880s on, particularly in New York and Chicago, changed the skyline of cities and gave the impression of cities of glass.

In *Caesar's Column* (1890), Ignatius Donnelly portrayed New York in 1988 as a huge city of ten million people, lit by harnessing the Earth's magnetism. The streets, pathways and railways are on many levels, domed over, and reached by elevators. There are electric trains with electric-powered airships as the main aerial transport. Hotels have lush glass-covered roof gardens and elevators the size of rooms. Compare this to *After London* (1885) by Richard Jefferies, where a series of catastrophes has led to people deserting the cities leaving London a tree-smothered ruin and the Thames a poisonous swamp.

Both images would compete in fiction, though the super-city, which we witness all around the globe today, not just in the USA but also in places such as Kuala Lumpur, Dubai, São Paulo, Shanghai and Hong Kong, remains the one most associated with science fiction.

H.G. Wells helped cement that image in *When the Sleeper Wakes* (1899). His London of 2100 is a city of tall buildings joined by moving walkways at all levels. There are ubiquitous Babble Machines that pronounce propaganda, personal monoplanes and supersonic airliners. The original serial version was illustrated by French artist Henri Lanos and it is the visual image of future cities that

makes an indelible impression. This is why it has lent itself so commandingly to the cinema, as remembered from the films *Metropolis* (1927) and *Just Imagine* (1930) – which also had some tempting personal aircars – through to *Blade Runner* (1982) and *Judge Dredd* (1995).

Metropolis has become symbolic of a future city, though the author of the novel, Thea von Harbou (the wife of director Fritz Lang), saw the city as allegorical, with the workers trapped in the depths of the city and the aristocratic elite living in pleasure palaces at the

top of buildings. The city thus became an icon not just of progress but also of oppression – the towering buildings trapping the individuals within.

That image has also remained popular. Robert Silverberg took it to another level in *The World Inside* (1971). In 2381 the world's population is 75 billion. The majority live in huge Urban Monads, 1000-storey-high buildings, each one an agglomeration of cities housing nearly a million people and structured according to status. Monads are constantly being built with enough room between them that they do not overshadow

" He went to the railings of the balcony and leant forward. . . . The place into which he looked was an aisle of Titanic buildings, curving away in a spacious sweep in either direction."—*Page* 45.

" Broken masses of metal projected dismally from the complex wreckage, vast masses of twisted cable dropped like tangled seaweed. . . . All about this great white pile was a ring of desolation."—*Page* 153.

Above Future Los Angeles as depicted in the film *Blade Runner* (1982), directed by Ridley Scott. The original images for the city were drawn up by Scott with Syd Mead.

Right Two of Henri Lanos's illustrations to H.G. Wells's *When the Sleeper Awakes* as it appeared when first serialised in *The Graphic* in 1899. The first shows Graham, the Sleeper, as he looks out over the city of London in the year 2100. The second shows the city destroyed after the revolution against the controlling elite.

012642.d.22

Frank R. Paul's concept of a future city painted for the 1955 World Science Fiction Convention book cover.

each other and so that they leave room for agriculture – although the world inside and that outside never meet. The world inside is decadent and highly regulated.

David Wingrove's extensive Chung Kuo series that began with *The Middle Kingdom* (1989), set in a Chinese-dominated future 200 years hence, similarly depicts vast mile-high, continent-spanning cities made of a new super plastic. There are 300 levels with the topmost reserved for society's elite, whilst the dregs of humanity survive at the bottom.

Vast planet-wide cities were a feature of the so-called Golden Age of magazine science fiction in the 1940s and 1950s, the best known being Trantor, the capital of the first Galactic Empire in Isaac Asimov's *Foundation* series. The entire metropolis, which filled the planet Trantor, was covered by domes and given over entirely to administration: the ultimate bureaucracy. Asimov depicted an Earth that had become almost a complete urban entity in *The Caves of Steel* (1954), the 'caves' being vast domed city complexes linked by subways so that no one need go outside, an expression of Asimov's own agoraphobia.

Just imagine. What would life be like in a city a mile high and covering almost the entire country? How would it be powered, cleaned, its occupants fed and disease prevented?

In contrast to fictional mega-cities are depictions of our existing cities that struggle to contain a growing population, such as in *Soylent Green* (1973), the film based on Harry Harrison's novel *Make Room! Make Room!* (1966). The novel was set in 1999 in New York, home to 35 million. Everyone struggles to acquire the dwindling resources. Looting is common and there is social disorder. The rich are virtually barricaded into their apartments. Overpopulation is central to *334* (1972) by Thomas M. Disch. Also set in New York, in 2025, this complex, episodic novel shows various interlinking lives in a decaying, drug- and birth-controlled, stratum of society.

Urban decay is the driving force in much of J.G. Ballard's later work. In *High Rise* (1975), the most intense of his urban novels, a modern high-rise apartment becomes a world unto itself, its occupants cutting themselves off from the rest of society, reverting to tribalism.

Bellona, the isolated city in Samuel R. Delany's *Dhalgren* (1975), is another urban complex that seems to generate its own existence. This long but fractured novel suggests a city that exists in tune with its psychologically damaged occupants, as if the city itself has had a mental breakdown. In *The City Dwellers* (1970; as *Twilight of the City*, 1977), Charles Platt explores the stress and psychological disorder that a city imposes upon its inhabitants, likening the city to a disease. The diseased city is a feature of cyberpunk, the quasi-genre that emerged in the 1980s depicting a concentrated urban future where the city has fused with advanced cybertechnology. John Shirley presaged this field with *City Come A-Walkin'* (1980), set in a near-future San Francisco, where the city has generated its own Overmind in order to protect itself from corrupt political control.

The transition from the old-style futuristic 'Metropolis' to the modern urban complex was marked by William Gibson in 'The Gernsback Continuum' (1981), where a photographer filming old, near-forgotten, future-style architecture is aware, briefly, of an alternate future where those cities continued and were not replaced by urban decadence.

Cities surviving through time is another strong image. On the fringes of science fiction is the unique gothic city-

China Miéville (born 1972)

English author whose works cross genres. Whilst much of it is defined as fantasy, it utilizes images from all aspects of imaginative and speculative literature, creating a style that he described as the 'New Weird'. At the heart of almost all his work is the city, most evident in the New Crobuzon series that began with *Perdido Street Station* (2000) and includes *The Scar* (2002) and *Iron Council* (2004). New Crobuzon is a city-state that might be seen to exist in a parallel medieval or even far-future Earth but with burgeoning Victorian technology – verging on 'steampunk'. Miéville has explored different aspects of London in *King Rat* (1998) and *Un Lun Dun* (2007), but his most complex urban portrayal is *The City & The City* (2009), a study of two cities in Eastern Europe that occupy much the same physical space, but whose inhabitants are conditioned to perceive only their own city. The cities have developed totally separate existences and any attempt to cross over is illegal and subject to the rigorous discipline of Breach, a form of inter-city secret police. The book appeared twenty years after the fall of the Berlin Wall and that association with all divided cities is potent. Miéville gives his cities depth, dimension and life, so that they are as much a character of his novels as the people.

Edward Miller's original cover artwork for *Perdido Street Station* by China Miéville.

castle of Gormenghast, which features in the trilogy by Mervyn Peake that began with *Titus Groan* (1946). The castle and its ruling family have existed for centuries, and both are falling into decay and ruin. There are echoes of Gormenghast in Viriconium, the dying city created by M. John Harrison in *The Pastel City* (1971); Cinnabar, the City at the Centre of Time, in *Cinnabar* (1976) by Edward Bryant; and New Crobuzon, created by China Miéville in *Perdido Street Station* (2000).

Miéville acknowledged the influence of both Peake and Harrison on his work.

Rome is known as the Eternal City, but in Arthur C. Clarke's *The City and the Stars* (1956) that city is Diaspar. A billion years in the future Diaspar is, so its few living occupants believe, the last city on Earth. It looks after its population, storing individuals' memories when they die and creating new bodies for them. It is the ultimate city.

Machine or Human?

When the Czech playwright, Karel Čapek, wrote his play *Rossumovi univerzální roboti* (*Rossum's Universal Robots*) in 1920, he used the word *robota* to describe the artificial workers that had been created in their millions to work as slaves across the world. *Robota* is a Czech word dating back to the seventeenth century meaning unpaid labour. The play was first produced in Prague in January 1921 and brought to New York in October 1922 and London in April 1923. The word was translated as robot and it rapidly passed into the English language. Our image of robots tends to be of mechanical men. In Čapek's play, the workers were synthetic, grown in vats, and though made in the likeness of men and women, were sexless. In science fiction these are usually called androids from an old word meaning 'man like'.

At the end of the play the robots rebel and wipe out mankind. They have developed sufficiently to have emotion and have supplanted humans in the next stage of evolution. It brings into focus the relationship between humans and machines and who might have supremacy.

Robots have their origins in the mechanical toys or automata of the Middle Ages. In 1206, the engineer Ibn Al-Jazari, long resident in Turkey, is believed to have created a programmable set of automata that played music. In 1495 Leonardo da Vinci designed a robot knight that responded to a drum beat. The most famous or notorious automaton was the chess-player known as the Turk, built by Wolfgang von Kempelen in 1769 and acquired by Johann Maelzel, who toured with it across Europe and

America. It was later proved to be a hoax, exposed by Edgar Allan Poe and others, but its fame inspired fiction, including two stories by German fantasist, E.T.A. Hoffmann, 'Automata' (1814) and 'Der Sandmann' ('The Sandman', 1816). The latter is the first example of a man being fooled into believing a female automaton is real and falls in love with her.

More significantly, the Turk turned Charles Babbage's thoughts to a mechanical calculator, which became the Difference Engine and began the long road to computers. This provides a link to 'cyborg' (cybernetic organism), the most recent, more specialist term. It relates to the augmentation of a human body by mechanical parts, a fusion of human and machine. It was coined in 1960, but came into popularity with the TV series *The Six*

Mʳ O. SMITH as the MONSTER.
in
FRANKENSTEIN.

London Pubᵈ by J. Duncombe, 19 Little Queen Street, Holborn

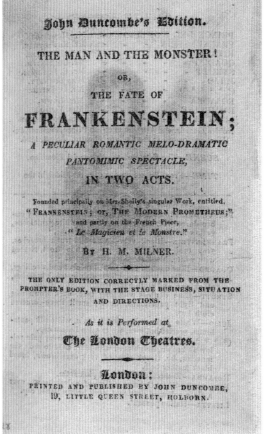

John Duncombe's Edition.

THE MAN AND THE MONSTER!

OR,

THE FATE OF

FRANKENSTEIN;

A PECULIAR ROMANTIC MELO-DRAMATIC
PANTOMIMIC SPECTACLE,

IN TWO ACTS.

Founded principally on Mrs. Shelly's singular Work, entitled,
"FRANKENSTEIN; or, THE MODERN PROMETHEUS;"
and partly on the French Piece,
"Le Magicien et le Monstre."

BY H. M. MILNER.

THE ONLY EDITION CORRECTLY MARKED FROM THE
PROMPTER'S BOOK, WITH THE STAGE BUSINESS, SITUATION
AND DIRECTIONS.

As it is Performed at
The London Theatres.

London:
PRINTED AND PUBLISHED BY JOHN DUNCOMBE,
19, LITTLE QUEEN STREET, HOLBORN.

The unnamed being created by Baron Frankenstein as portrayed in the melodrama, *The Man and the Monster; or, the Fate of Frankenstein* (1852) by Henry M. Milner adapted from Mary Shelley's novel. It was first performed in 1826 with Richard John 'O' Smith, who was renowned for playing villains and murderers, as the creature. Brian W. Aldiss declared *Frankenstein* 'the first real novel of science fiction.' (*Billion Year Spree*, 1973).
2304.a.1

Right Cover for the original
Polish edition of Stanislaw Lem's
Cyberiada (Krakow, 1965)
illustrated by Daniel Mróz.
X.908/6139

Below The original British
production of Karel Čapek's *R.U.R.*,
depicted in the *Illustrated London
News* for 12 May 1923.
LON LD47 NPL

Frontispiece to *The Island of Dr Moreau* by H.G. Wells (Heinemann, 1896). Illustration by C.R.A. Stone.
012627.L.2

" I could not distinguish what he said."

Page 60

Million Dollar Man (1973–8), based on Martin Caidin's book *Cyborg* (1972). The Daleks in *Dr Who* are thus cyborgs, as are the Borg in *Star Trek: The Next Generation*.

The idea of machine-enhanced human capability dates back at least to 1879 in 'The Ablest Man in the World' by Edward Page Mitchell. An inventor designs a miniature logic machine, like Babbage's, and implants it in the head of a man of low IQ. It converts him into a genius. Earlier, in 'The Man That was Used Up' (1839), Edgar Allan Poe described an army general who had been so badly injured that his body was made up entirely of spare parts.

The progenitor of all these stories was *Frankenstein, or The Modern Prometheus*

(1818) by Mary Shelley. She was intrigued by the idea of electricity as a life force, as suggested by Luigi Galvani. The creature created by Baron Frankenstein is made up of other body parts, a forerunner of genetic engineering, so is not a real robot or android. Instead, it goes to the heart of the extent to which these creations are human. Physicality aside, robots and androids are distinguished from humans because they have no emotions, they are not self-aware and cannot reproduce sexually. Furthermore being a machine, they would have no morals. The idea that a robot might endanger its creator has become known as the Frankenstein complex.

By the time of Čapek's *R.U.R.*, writers had already considered robots

Just imagine. Could mechanical life ever supersede humans? Could a machine ever be programmed with a soul or emotions and, if so, would that make it human?

Isaac Asimov (1920–92)

American writer of science fiction, mysteries and popular science, born in Byelorussia. Although the author of over 500 books, he is probably best remembered for his robot stories which began with 'Strange Playfellow' (1940). Following discussion with John W. Campbell, Jr, editor of *Astounding Science Fiction* magazine, Asimov developed the Three Laws of Robotics, which were first expounded in 'Liar!' (1941) and 'Runaround' (1942). In 'Liar!' a telepathic robot lies to humans so as not to hurt their feelings, but when it learns that lies also hurt feelings the robot is in a dilemma it cannot resolve and closes down. In 'Runaround' a robot finds itself trapped between conflicting demands of the Second and Third Laws, which can only be overcome by a human placing himself in danger so that the First Law overrides. For the next fifty years Asimov found ways of manipulating the laws to provide many permutations for stories, collected in *I, Robot* (1950) and more comprehensively in *The Complete Robot* (1982). Of special significance is 'The Bicentennial Man' (1976), later expanded as *The Positronic Man* (1993) with Robert Silverberg. A creative robot seeks to become human and gradually replaces robotic parts with organic ones, effectively becoming a cyborg in reverse, but only ultimately discovers the true nature of being human with its own death. Asimov wrote two novels, *The Caves of Steel* (1954) and *The Naked Sun* (1957), in which robot R. Daneel Olivaw assists a human, Elijah Baley, in solving two complicated crimes. After *The Robots of Dawn* (1983), Asimov developed a link between his robot stories and his Foundation series with *Robots and Empire* (1985) in which R. Daneel Olivaw has a crucial role. This includes augmenting the First Law so that robots not only protect humans but all humanity.

The tribute issue of *Asimov's Science Fiction*, November 1992, cover by Michael Whelan for 'A Robot's Farewell to the Master'.

---

that take on human characteristics, humans that become part or almost all mechanical, or humans that are rebuilt. All these developments challenge the definition of human.

Science fiction has addressed these issues, most famously, as regards robots, by Isaac Asimov, who devised the Three Laws of Robotics.

1. A robot may not injure a human being or, through inaction, allow a human being to come to harm.
2. A robot must obey orders given to it by a human being except where such orders would conflict with the First Law.
3. A robot must protect its own existence as long as such

protection does not conflict with the First or Second Law.

Jack Williamson took Asimov's First Law to an extreme in *The Humanoids* (1949), when robots bring society to a halt by stopping humans doing anything that might be construed as harmful. Stanislaw Lem avoided any thought of robot laws in his satirical and often amusing stories that make up *Bajki robotów* (translated as *Mortal Engines*, 1964) and *Cyberiada* (*The Cyberiad*, 1965). Lem's robots, which are human in just about every respect except they need not die, have amazing technical skills but are frequently mischievous.

Philip K. Dick, perhaps the most paranoid of all science-fiction writers, often considered the difference between

robots and humans. In 'Impostor' (1953), a man is accused of being an android replicant that has planted a bomb. He tries to prove his innocence, but the bomb is programmed to explode at the moment he realizes he is not human. Dick developed the idea in *Do Androids Dream of Electric Sheep?* (1968), adapted for the cinema as *Blade Runner* (1982), where a police bounty hunter is tracking down renegade androids that are human in all respects except they lack empathy.

Some of the most intriguing stories are those that study a robot society. *Code of the Lifemaker* (1983) by James P. Hogan considers how alien self-replicating robots, which landed on Titan millennia ago, might evolve and react to humans. In Brian W. Aldiss's 'But Who Can Replace a Man?'

(1958), robots with varying degrees of intelligence club together after the report of man's extinction, but have little idea of what to do until they meet a human. In 'Robot's Return' (1938), Robert Moore Williams has robots return to Earth seeking their creator and finding it unbelievable that it was something as frail as humans.

The cyborg overcomes the frailty of humans. In their play *Blood and Iron* (1917), Perley Poore Sheehan and Robert H. Davis have wounded soldiers rebuilt with mechanical parts, making them stronger. Their human emotions remain and one of them succeeds in killing the Kaiser. Early 'cyborg' stories usually provide a mechanical body to supplement the human. This often took the form of human brains in robot bodies, of which arguably the best story was 'No Woman Born' (1934) by C.L. Moore. She describes a dancer injured in a fire. Her brain is transplanted to a robot body, which significantly improves her dancing skills. An unusual story from the early magazines is 'The Artificial Man' (1929) by Clare Winger Harris in which an athlete loses a leg and has an artificial replacement. He later loses an arm and becomes so depressed that he undergoes operations to have all his limbs and organs replaced by artificial ones.

The Russian writer Aleksandr Beliaev, who was himself paralyzed in later life, wrote several novels involving transplanted body parts. *Golova professor Douela* (*Professor Dowell's Head*, 1925) not only has a disembodied head kept alive, but also transplants the head of a female dancer onto the body of a dead singer. *Chelovek amfibiya* (as *The Amphibian*, 1928) has an injured child survive through the transplant of shark's gills, which means the boy grows up amphibious.

The concept of cyborgs has evolved alongside the idea of genetic engineering, a term used by Jack Williamson in *Dragon's Island* (1951), where scientists seek to create new forms of life. Its forerunner was *The Island of Dr Moreau* (1896), where H.G. Wells has his scientist conduct surgery on animals seeking to adapt them into humans. Science fiction has been most interested in how science might adapt humans to live in other environments. Olaf Stapledon considered this in *Last and First Men* (1930), where humans are adapted to exist on Venus and Neptune. James Blish coined the word 'pantropy' to describe this type of adaptation for the stories later collected as *The Seedling Stars* (1957). Frederik Pohl's *Man Plus* (1976) brings us full circle by having a man modified into a cyborg so as to survive on Mars. Human and robot elements might also be adapted into other non-human forms, such as spaceships in Anne McCaffrey's *The Ship Who Sang* (1969).

Bruce Sterling brought all these developments together in his Shaper stories, which began in 1982 with 'Spider Rose' and include the collection *Crystal Express* (1989) and the novel *Schismatrix* (1985). As space is colonized humans split into two groups. The Shapers prefer genetic or organic manipulation, including selective breeding, to adapt the body to life in space. The Mechanists prefer cybernetic enhancement, including computer simulation.

The extent to which we readily augment our actions in computer games using Wii technology shows our willingness to adapt to new developments. Similarly the comic-book hero Iron Man, created by Stan Lee in 1963, has a powered exoskeleton that provides prodigious strength, and similar outfits are being developed by the military. How soon will it be before we can no longer distinguish human from machine?

The cyborg from the film *Iron Man* (2008). Artwork by Adi Granov.

The Singularity

In a talk given in 1993, science-fiction writer Vernor Vinge said: 'Within thirty years, we will have the technological means to create superhuman intelligence. Shortly after, the human era will be ended.'

Vinge suggested that the developments of the last few decades in computer technology, the internet, the computer-human relationship and bio-technology could create a point at which a computer intelligence would be created that is vastly superior to human intelligence. He called this point the Technological Singularity (now referred to simply as the Singularity)suggesting that once it is reached, scientific progress will become so rapid, driven by these new intelligences, that humankind will be left far behind. Damien Broderick used the word 'spike' to describe the same moment in *The Spike* (1997). Contributing to 'the spike' are developments in nanotechnology,

creating infinitely smaller machines that can undertake bio-engineering, another aspect of the human-machine interface.

In 1950, the wartime computer-pioneer and code breaker, Alan Turing devised a test to determine whether we could tell the difference between a human intelligence responding to questions typed into a computer terminal and a sophisticated computer programme. He suspected that by the year 2000 most computers would fool the investigator into believing the responses were from a human.

Aspects of the Singularity had featured for some years in science fiction. Fredric Brown wonderfully presaged it in his 250-word vignette 'Answer' (1954), when all the computers across the Galaxy are connected with the throw of a switch, at which point a new god comes into existence. There are similar stories by Isaac Asimov, 'The Last

Question' (1956) and Arthur C. Clarke, 'Dial F for Frankenstein' (1965). Tim Berners-Lee later revealed that Clarke's story, where a vast telephone network becomes sentient, was one of the triggers behind him developing the internet. Algis Budrys also presaged the internet in *Michaelmas* (1977) through a programme he calls Domino, which developed into a sentient investigative computer.

One of the best-known early examples of nanotechnology is the film *Fantastic Voyage* (1966), where a submarine and its crew are miniaturized in order to enter the body of a scientist in a coma and clear a blood clot in the brain. There is a much earlier example in *Travels in the Interior* (1887) by Alfred Taylor Schofield, although this tour of the human body from the inside is little more than a disguised lecture. Maurice Renard's *Un Homme chez les microbes* (A Man Among the Microbes, 1928) might have been a more

Vernor Vinge (born 1944)

American writer, computer scientist and professor of mathematics. He has been writing science fiction since 1965. His early novels, starting with *Grimm's World* (1969), were fairly traditional planetary adventures, but this changed with *True Names* (1981), a pioneering story about the manipulation of cyberspace. Then came *The Peace War* (1984) and its sequel *Marooned in Realtime* (1986). They follow the creation of a stasis field, the 'bobble', in which time stands still. Those who use a bobble to travel into the future discover an unpopulated Earth with all humanity having vanished in the twenty-third century. This is Vinge's first hint of the Singularity and its effect on Earth's population. After a couple of space-quest novels, *A Fire Upon the Deep* (1992) and *A Deepness in the Sky* (1999), Vinge returned to the Singularity in *Rainbow's End* (2006), which considers the rapidly increasing growth in technology, particularly augmented reality.

'*Marooned in Real Time*' serialized in *Analog*, as depicted on the May 1986 issue, cover by Tom Kidd. It depicts the time stasis bobble by which a remnant of humanity survived the Singularity.

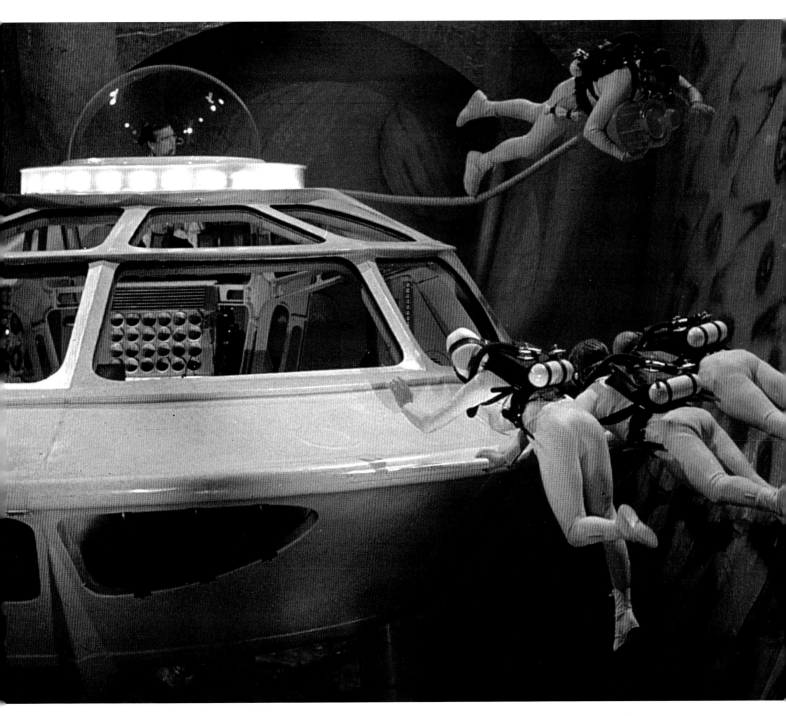

Scene from *Fantastic Voyage* (1966), directed by Richard Fleischer, showing scientists travelling through the bloodstream.

Just imagine. Could you be certain that the answers to your emails are from a human rather than a machine? What questions would you ask to be sure?

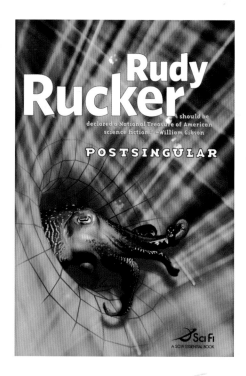

Postsingular (2007) by Rudy Rucker. Perhaps the ultimate post-Singularity novel. An eccentric scientist infests the Earth with billions of quantum-computing nanomachines which create life forms that pyramid into a superhuman planetary mind. The Earth and everything that is in it comes alive.

Right A nanorobot with blood cells depicted by Christian Darkin.

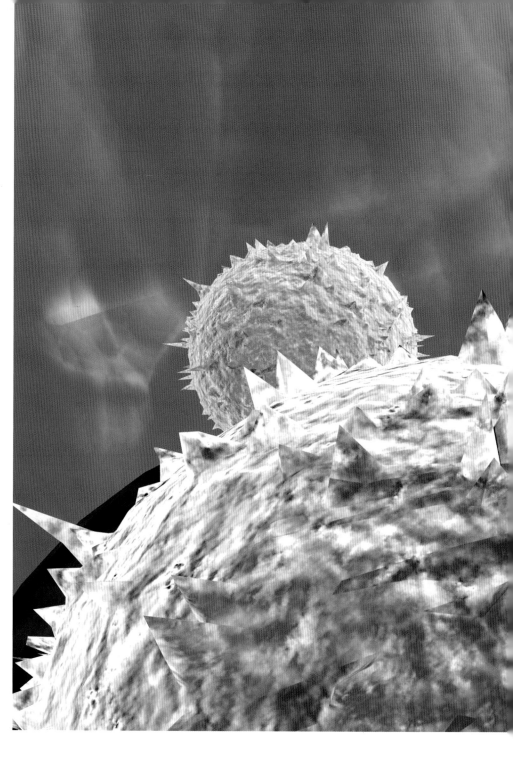

relevant precursor, had not Renard revised it to become simply a journey to a utopian world amongst the infinitely small.

Philip E. High foresaw nanotechnology in *These Savage Futurians* (1967), describing a series of machines making increasingly smaller machines until a micro-robot can be injected into the body to tackle infection. There is a similar set-up in Barry Malzberg's *The Men Inside* (1972), though in his world the micro-surgeons turn killers.

These twin threads of computer intelligence and nanotechnology came together in *Blood Music* (1985) by Greg Bear. A biotechnologist transforms RNA molecules into biological computers. When he injects them into his own bloodstream these rapidly multiply and conjoin as a sentient hive mind. They soon outstrip their host and multiply across the planet.

Bear had presaged what became called the 'grey goo' hypothesis by Eric Drexler in *Engines of Creation* (1986), where

he proposed that 'nanobots' would rapidly multiply through basic raw materials and could destroy the Earth within days. Similar nanobot threats appear in *Prey* (2002) by Michael Crichton, whilst in *Bloom* (1998) by Wil McCarthy, Earth has already been destroyed and the nanobots, called Mycora, threaten the rest of the solar system. Kathleen Ann Goonan's Nanotech Plague series, which began with *Queen City Jazz* (1994), takes us on a tour of an Earth devastated by nanotechnology. The Melding

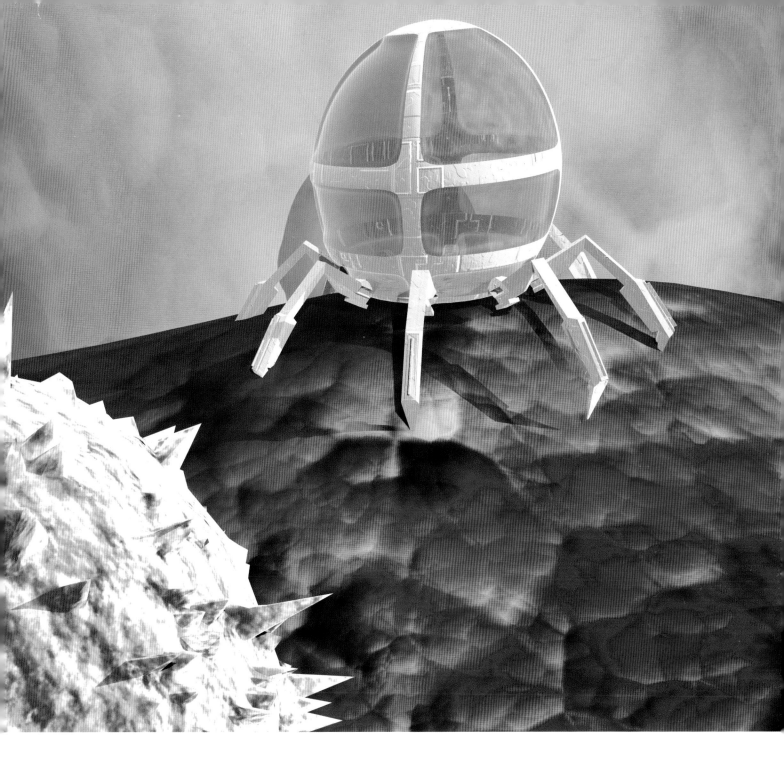

Plague in Alastair Reynolds's Revelation Space series is another nanotech virus, seen at its worst in *Chasm City* (2001).

Charles Stross has provided two approaches to the Singularity. In *Singularity Sky* (2003) there is a super-intelligent AI from the future, called Eschaton, which communicates with our present with a warning that no one will violate causality or it will seek retribution. Although Eschaton claims it is not God, it has nevertheless taken control of the Universe in order to protect itself and the future. In the sequence of stories that were collected as *Accelerando* (2005), Stross follows the generations of a family as they cope with a series of technological Singularities that drives humanity to the stars.

There can be little doubt that the pace of development of new technologies will continue to accelerate and that the future will see rapid and increasingly more bewildering changes. The great challenge to mankind is how it will cope.

Far Futures

The Earth is about 4.6 billion years old and is expected to survive perhaps another 7 billion years before it is absorbed into an expanding Sun entering its Red Dwarf stage. Life on Earth will already be extinct, maybe 4 billion years from now.

It is still a very long time, far longer than life has already existed on Earth, which is about 1,000 million years. Plenty of time for humans and animals to evolve beyond recognition, for continents to have drifted and reformed, for humans to have reached a scientific peak and have left the planet altogether to find new homes across the Galaxy.

In 1893, H.G. Wells wrote an essay, 'The Man of the Year Million', in which he proposed that as humans will rely more on their brain than their body, their heads will become very large and their bodies small, barely able to support the head, so that they crawl around on all fours, relying on various means of transport. Eden Phillpotts responded with 'A Story Without an End' (in *Fancy Free*, 1901) where he describes the man of the year million as pliable, pink with a cone-like head, wings, gills and telepathic.

H.G. Wells depicted the Earth's last days at the end of *The Time Machine* (1895), when the Traveller ventures 30 million years into the future to see a cold, dark world, with no more day and night, silent except for the wind, and lifeless except for a round, flopping thing with tentacles. His vision of a frozen Earth was picked up by the artist Warwick Goble who depicted it symbolically for a feature, 'How Will the World End?' (1900) (see page 118).

Whatever happens in the far future, it will seem completely alien. Arthur C. Clarke's Third Law of Prediction states: 'Any sufficiently advanced technology is indistinguishable from magic.' As a consequence many stories of Earth's last days are as much fantasy as they are science fiction, such as *The Dying Earth* (1950) by Jack Vance or the Zothique cycle of stories by Clark Ashton Smith, posthumously collected in *Zothique* (1970). Michael

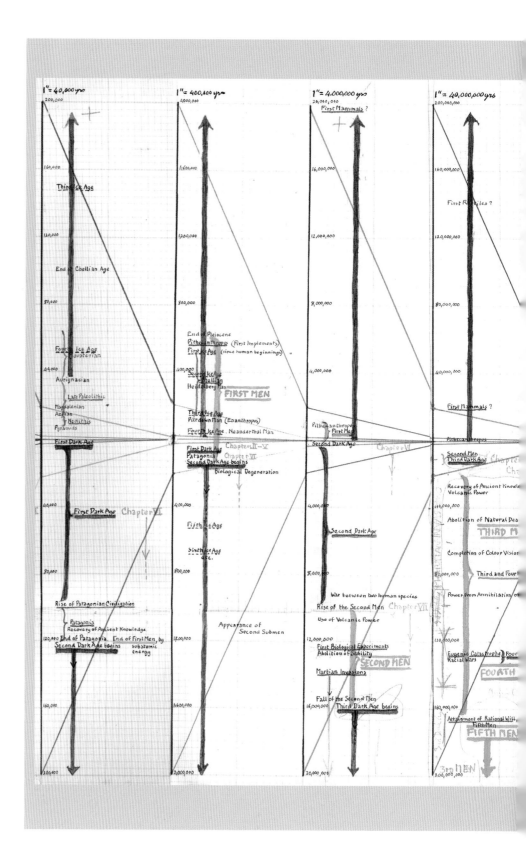

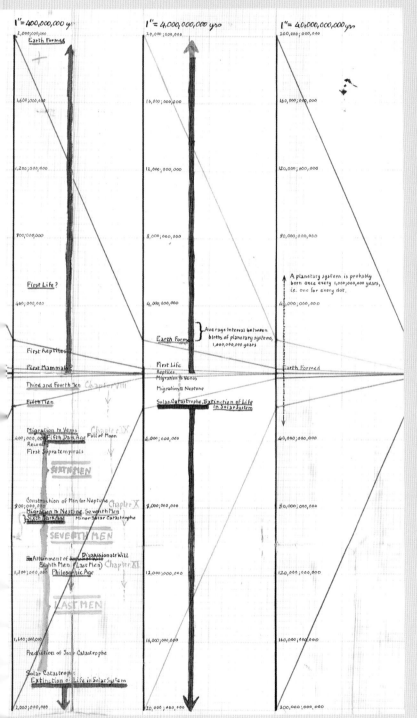

Olaf Stapledon (1886–1950)

British philosopher, writer and visionary. Stapledon turned to
fiction late in life after formulating his own personal philosophies in
A Modern Theory of Ethics (1929). He followed this with *Last and First
Men* (1930), which has the Last Man look back over eighteen waves
of evolution of humans during the last 2 billion years since the First
Man – which is ourselves. The time of the First Man is one of conflict
until a World State is established in 2300, with the Americans and
Chinese dominant. When the Earth's natural resources are depleted
bacterial warfare follows, which wipes out most of the human race.
It is a hundred millennia before a new race of humans emerges from
Patagonia. This one destroys itself through atomic warfare and ten
million years pass before Second Man emerges, who are far more
altruistic but they are subject to constant attack from Mars, and
when a virus is released to combat the Martians it also wipes out the
humans. Stapledon continues through each generation of humans.
Third Man is catlike with enhanced senses, Fourth Man is telepathic,
Fifth Man realizes the Moon will disintegrate and so migrates to
Venus, which they adapt for human life. Stapledon moves on. Ninth
Man migrates to Neptune but does not survive. Earth struggles
through millions of years until Fifteenth Man emerges to create a great
and lasting civilization. Fifteenth Man genetically creates Sixteenth
Man and so on to Eighteenth Man, which takes on many forms.
They are the Last Men because the Sun is about to explode and they
broadcast their seed through space. The Last Men can travel back
through time and in a mini-sequel, *Last Men in London* (1932), one of
them makes contact with a First Man at the time of World War I. The
two billion years of Earth's history becomes but a passing moment in
Star Maker (1937), which covers a hundred billion years across the
Universe and identifies some of the later genera of Men. Enhanced
intelligence and superior intellect are explored in two other novels:
Odd John (1935), about a superman, and *Sirius* (1944), about an
intelligent dog.

Part of Olaf Stapledon's original
future timeline chart he prepared
for *Last and First Men* (1930).

Moorcock wrote a sequence of novels, later combined in an omnibus as *The Dancers at the End of Time* (1981), which depicts Earth in its last days when entropy has fulfilled its function and the universe is collapsing. Earth's final inhabitants live a decadent lifestyle, uncaring of their circumstances. They create their own illusory landscape around them as the world is otherwise a sterile wilderness. Other books with a rather dreamy, resigned atmosphere include *The 100th Millennium* (1959) by John Brunner, *Midsummer Century* (1972) by James Blish and *The Celestial Steam Locomotive* (1983) and its sequel by Michael G. Coney.

Perhaps the most unusual image of the Earth's last days – unique in all science fiction – is in *The Night Land* (1912) by William Hope Hodgson. Millions of years in the future the Sun has died and Earth's inhabitants survive with heat and power from the 'earth-current' and volcanic eruptions. Most of humanity lives in a huge pyramid and discovers that another remnant survive in a smaller pyramid. One man sets out across the hostile land to rescue them. The land is inhabited by the strangest creatures, descendants of biological experiments in millennia past. Hodgson's future vision is unequalled, but the story is spoiled by his use of a pseudo-archaic language.

Other unusual far-future visions include the stories that make up *Hothouse* (1962) by Brian W. Aldiss. Earth is locked in rotation with one face to the Sun, and the planet is covered entirely by vegetation. Humans have shrunk in size and insects and small creatures survive, but most other animals are extinct. Giant spiders have spun cobwebs between the Earth and Moon. In *A Billion Days of Earth* (1976), Doris Piserchia depicts a noisome far future where humans have evolved into decadent god-like creatures, rats have become the new humans, and a new creature comes into existence that determines to cleanse the Earth.

The image of a dying, decadent Earth is one that evokes much sense of wonder. John W. Campbell, Jr, who had been renowned for his extravagant space operas, changed mood completely and, writing under the alias Don A. Stuart, wrote 'Twilight' (1934) and 'Night' (1935). 'Twilight' describes Earth

THE MAN OF THE YEAR MILLION.

millions of years in the future. Almost all life is extinct and the few humans who remain (others have settled on Neptune) live in automated cities run by machines. By the time of 'Night', all humans are extinct, the universe is collapsing and only a few machines remain on Neptune awaiting the end.

Campbell may well have been inspired by the work of British writer Olaf Stapledon, who had chronicled the future history of humanity over the next 2 billion years in *Last and First Men* (1930). Stapledon's soaring vision, which he took even further in *Star Maker* (1937), has never been equalled in science fiction, and shows the enormous span of time in which humanity has to evolve. Conflicts and troubles that concern us today are as nothing in the eternity of the universe and we are still learning, mere infants on a cosmic scale.

FLOOER
Florifacies mirabila

The flooer has glands around its mouth that produce a sweet-smelling secretion that is attractive to insects.

The night stalker's powerful front legs are developed from the wings of its ancestors. Its back feet, which were originally used for grasping and clutching, now come over its shoulders and effectively form hands.

NIGHT STALKER
Manambulus perhorridus

Left H.G. Wells's essay 'The Man of the Year Million' as it appeared in the *Pall Mall Budget*, 16 November, 1893.
LON 443 NPL

Right The Flooer and Night Stalker are both distant descendants of bats, fifty million years hence, as depicted in 'After Man' (1981) by Dougal Dixon.
L.42/1332

Just imagine. What form will humans take in a million or a billion years' time, or will humans exist at all? Might an animal evolve and prove superior? If so, which one?

The End of the World

There are many ancient traditions of a final apocalypse – the biblical Armageddon, the Norse Ragnarök, the Islamic Yawm ad-Din. The earliest work of secular fiction to depict the end of the world, *Le Dernier Homme* (*The Last Man*, 1805) by Jean-Baptiste Cousin de Grainville, drew upon biblical imagery. It looked at a storm-wracked, sterile world where the last man and woman choose to have no children and thereby end this 'system of things'.

There have been several occasions in Earth's 4.6-billion year history when almost all life on Earth has been wiped out. The best known was the extinction of the dinosaurs, about 65 million years ago, when a meteor struck the Earth. There was a period known as Snowball Earth, around 700 million years ago, when the entire surface of the Earth froze over. The worst catastrophe, known as the Great Dying, happened about 250 million years ago when a combination of massive volcanic action and collision with an asteroid about the size of Mount Everest wiped out about 90 per cent of all life.

Earth encounters cosmic dust every day – it is what causes 'shooting stars'. But there are many much larger objects that could cause massive devastation if they struck the Earth. In 1989 the Earth was narrowly missed by a 340-metre wide asteroid that passed through the exact spot where Earth had been six hours before.

Many of these near-Earth objects are known and tracked, but smaller ones may only be detected within days of approaching Earth. The end of life on Earth therefore remains a possibility at any time from these near-Earth objects or any other cosmic disaster.

Beside cosmic disasters there is the potential for other natural or man-made disasters. Climate change may lead to a new Ice Age or a desert Earth, bringing with it rising sea levels, storms, famine and plague. Plagues or pandemics may arise regardless of climate change. The most devastating was the bubonic plague of the mid-fourteenth century, later called the Black Death, which killed perhaps half the population of Europe and reduced the world's population by over 75 million.

The threat of overpopulation remains. The world's population has risen from 1.6 billion in 1900 to around 6.7 billion at present, with an estimate approaching 10 billion by 2050. Projections for how much the Earth's natural resources can sustain such a population vary, but the twenty-first century will be critical to resolving the problems.

Finally, if nature does not wipe out civilization, mankind has the capacity, through nuclear or biological warfare, to destroy itself.

This section looks at how science fiction has considered these doomsday scenarios and at how humanity might survive.

Right David Hardy's painting *Yucatan* depicts the asteroid striking the Earth that brought about the end of the dinosaurs.

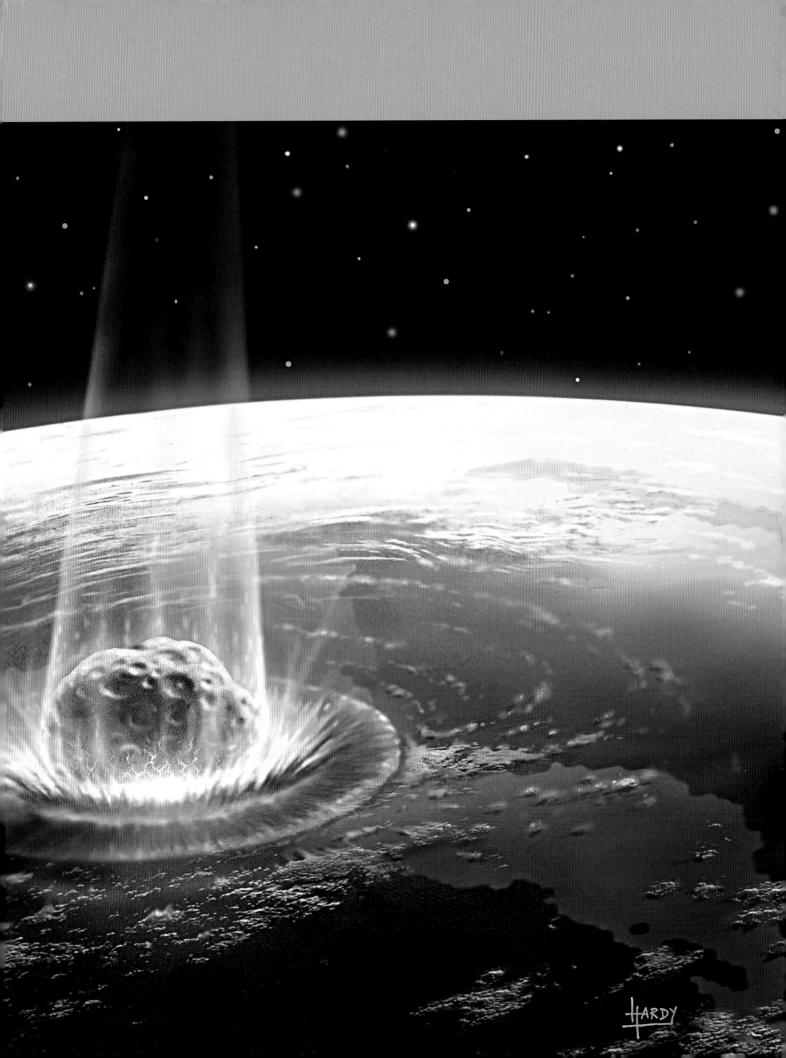

The first science-fiction disaster novel was Mary Shelley's *The Last Man* (1826), which was born out of her grief and frustration at the death of her children, her husband and her close friends. At the end of the twenty-first century a virulent plague sweeps round the world. Britain tries to isolate itself, but as the population dwindles the last survivors cross Europe hoping to find a haven. One by one they die and the last heads off alone.

Plagues such as cholera and typhoid were endemic in Shelley's day. The nineteenth century saw a growing awareness of the link between plagues and pollution. Naturalist Richard Jefferies's *After London* (1885) was the first major novel to consider the triumph of nature over industrialization when, after an unexplained catastrophe, Britain returns to a primitive state. Earlier, in *The Doom of the Great City* (1880), William DeLisle Hay had shown London's population suffocating from excessive smog. By the turn of the century there were many stories showing people's fears of pollution. Fred M. White's series 'The Doom of London' (1903) subjects the city to a sequence of catastrophes from blizzards to fire to an epidemic caused by pollution.

In *The Purple Cloud* (1901), M.P. Shiel wipes out humanity when a poisonous gas erupts from a volcano and spreads round the world. He follows the odyssey of the last man who escaped death because he had been at the North Pole. He spends twenty years alone, becoming increasingly mad, until he discovers the last surviving woman.

A plague called the Scarlet Death wipes out all but a few hundred souls in Jack London's *The Scarlet Plague* (1914). People revert to tribalism, and the faults of civilization – greed, lust for power, selfishness – continue. Man never learns.

The classic plague novel is *Earth Abides* (1949) by George R. Stewart, in which an airborne virus kills almost everyone. The book follows one survivor, the ecologically aware Ish, who travels across

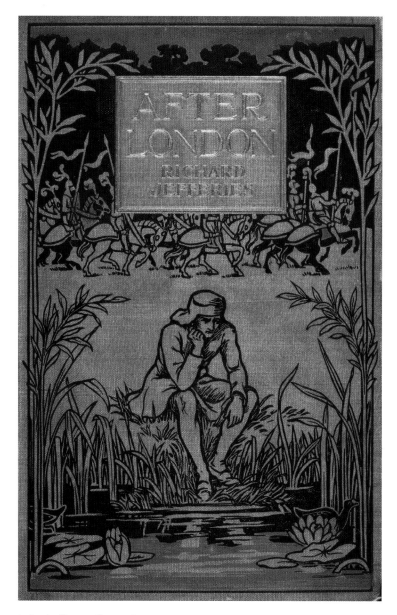

Richard Jefferies, *After London* (1885).
012622.h.22

Just imagine. The natural urge to escape a plague is to retreat to an isolated position and hope the plague doesn't reach you. But where? How do you survive while you wait and how do you know when it's safe to emerge?

Above William DeLisle Hay, *The Doom of the Great City* (1880).

Top right John Ames Mitchell, *The Last American* (1889). This tongue-in-cheek but pessimistic forecast suggests that by 1990 the United States will cease to exist, pulled apart by too many racial, religious and cultural differences. A Persian expedition in 2951 explores the ruins of New York and Washington and finds the last surviving American.
012705.ee.27

Right John Brunner, *The Sheep Look Up* (Harper, 1972). Artwork by Mark Rubin.

North America, witnessing small, doomed pockets of survivors. On his return he finds a woman survivor and they raise a family. The children, not knowing the old world, are perfectly at home with an increasingly primitive lifestyle. Ish accepts that civilization has gone and hopes the new world will not make the same mistakes.

A rather more unusual plague novel is *I Am Legend* (1954) by Richard Matheson, filmed in 2007, in which a bacterium that can infect both the living and the dead converts all humanity into vampires except for one lone human.

The Death of Grass (1956) by John Christopher introduces a virus that destroys all grasses, including rice and cereal crops. It begins in Asia. Europe remains complacent that an anti-virus will be found so no one is prepared when the plague reaches Britain. Christopher shows how rapidly the social order breaks down and how futile governments are to respond.

Christopher's book was a return to ecological concerns. There had been earlier stories. In *Nordenholt's Million* (1923) by J.J. Connington, a mutated bacterium escapes and wipes out all vegetation. In 'The Man Who Hated Flies' (1929) by J.D. Beresford, a man invents the perfect insecticide but when applied it disrupts pollination leading to crop failure and famine. At the other extreme, *Greener Than You Think* (1947) by Ward Moore shows how a formula to improve plant growth runs amok, and before long the Earth is suffocated by vegetation. It was bio-engineering of plants that created the triffids in *The Day of the Triffids* (1951) by John Wyndham. All these books preceded the groundbreaking *Silent Spring* (1962) by Rachel Carson, which raised government awareness to the environmental damage caused by pesticides, notably DDT. Pollution returned as a major theme.

In *The Burning World* (1964; revised as *The Drought*) by J.G. Ballard, radioactive waste coats the surface of the oceans and interrupts the natural water cycle, stopping rain. Humanity clusters along the coast and, as in Christopher's novel, there is growing anarchy.

The classic novel of pollution is *The Sheep Look Up* (1972) by John Brunner, set in a not-too-distant future when American industry dictates to the White House. The

John Wyndham (1903–69)

Pseudonym of British writer John Beynon Harris, best remembered as the author of *The Day of the Triffids* (1951) and other disaster novels. Wyndham sold stories under his real name and other pseudonyms to the science-fiction pulps starting in 1931, but in 1950 he reinvented himself as John Wyndham and became one of the world's best-selling science-fiction writers with a series of catastrophe novels. In *The Day of the Triffids*, a particularly vivid meteor shower blinds almost everyone on Earth. As mankind struggles to survive, the few sighted ones have to combat the growing menace of the triffids, bio-engineered walking, carnivorous plants. In *The Kraken Wakes* (1953), aliens land and settle in the depths of the oceans, but when man seeks to destroy them they retaliate by melting the ice caps and flooding most of the Earth. *The Chrysalids* (1955) is set many centuries after a nuclear war when mutations arising from radiation begin to manifest with telepathic powers. Wyndham developed the idea in *The Midwich Cuckoos* (1957), filmed as *Village of the Damned* (1960), where children are born in a small village by some form of alien impregnation. As they mature they bond together and protect themselves by mind control. *Web* (1979) was published posthumously and lacks the usual Wyndham polish. It reveals that the new menace facing the Earth is a deadly strain of intelligent spider that evolved after nuclear testing. Wyndham's books were called 'cosy' catastrophes by Brian Aldiss, but this reflects Wyndham's style rather than the nature of the catastrophes – which in all his books are extremely unpleasant.

Poster for the 1962 film adaptation of John Wyndham's *The Day of the Triffids*, directed by the Hungarian film director Steve Sekely.

government refuses to recognize links with pollution that is killing life in the sea, causing widespread disease and mutations and changing the weather systems.

Science fiction continues to explore the extent to which viruses can be manipulated by humans. *Oryx and Crake* (2003) by Margaret Atwood looks at a world already spiralling towards disaster, with mass extinction arising from climate change when a man-made virus leaks out into society and kills almost

everyone. Her post-apocalyptic world is bleak and unyielding, though some hope is offered in the book's partner novel, *The Year of the Flood* (2009), where a small religious sect look to the future.

What all these novels have in common is science's lack of control over the creation of new bacteria, how ill-prepared governments are to respond to any major catastrophe and how rapidly social decay occurs, as if civilization is but a thin veneer.

Perils from Space

Full hot and high the sea would boil,
Full red the forests gleam

These lines form part of the poem 'The Comet' (1832) by American physician and poet Oliver Wendell Holmes, Sr., who was the first to give serious thought to the consequences of a comet striking the Earth. The narrator witnesses total destruction following futile attempts to destroy the comet by shooting at it. Earlier, in *Les Posthumes* (1802), Rétif de la Bretonne had considered the floods that would arise when a comet passes so close to the Earth that it becomes a second moon.

Events in the heavens have long been regarded as harbingers of doom, particularly solar eclipses or the appearance of a comet. In 1705, Edmund Halley calculated the orbit of the comet now named after him and predicted its return in 1758 (though he was not around to see it), but this assurance did not remove the fear that a comet might collide with the Earth.

The return of Halley's Comet in 1835 revived interest. In 'The Conversation of Eiros and Charmion' (1839), Edgar Allan Poe showed that a comet need not collide to be fatal. A comet passing near Earth sucks the nitrogen from the atmosphere leaving pure oxygen which ignites. 'The Comet' (1838) by the otherwise unknown S. Austin, Jr, shows how a cometary collision may only be calculated accurately in the last few days. This allows the author time to reflect, but offers little chance of averting the danger. In Austin's story the characters

'The End of the Moon' as depicted by Frank R. Paul
in *Science Fiction Plus*, August 1953.

await the last moment questioning whether this is God's intervention.

Cosmic doom can be used to promote religious zeal and explore the human conscience. A religious fanatic does just that in *The Crack of Doom* (1886) by William Minto. The comet does not strike the Earth but it serves its purpose in allowing the fanatic to manipulate the situation. H.G. Wells explored similar territory in 'The Star' (1897), where a rogue planetoid collides with Neptune creating a new star that heads towards Earth. Although the worst excesses are reduced by the Moon intervening and sheltering the Earth, there are gravitational effects that cause floods and earthquakes destroying most of humanity; but Wells sees a new and better world emerging. He repeated his thoughts in *In the Days of the Comet* (1906), where the gas from the comet brings euphoria to Earth and a rise in altruism.

George Griffith's 'The Great Crellin Comet' (1897), which appeared the same month as 'The Star', is important as the first story where a scientist constructs a giant gun to fire a projectile to divert the comet, in which he succeeds. It is also the first story to have a countdown from ten to one to mark the launch.

The Canadian astronomer Simon Newcomb held out no such hope in 'The End of the World' (1903). He has an object collide with the Sun, which explodes and the heat devastates the Earth. A few who hide in a deep shelter emerge to a sterile wasteland. The same happens in

'Finis' (1906) by another Canadian writer, Frank Lillie Pollock. A scientist deduces there is a vast central universal sun and that when its heat reaches Earth it will destroy the planet. He calculates the day and the scientist and his fiancée await the final moment. There are several short but effective stories based on the simple idea of couples facing the inevitable, as in 'The Last Night of the World' (1951) by Ray Bradbury, 'Inconstant Moon' (1971) by Larry Niven and 'The Last Sunset' (1996) by Geoffrey A. Landis.

Most of the ideas relating to a comet or meteor striking the Earth had been explored by the early 1900s, and though later books may be more detailed – such as *Sixty Days to Live* (1939) by Dennis Wheatley or *Lucifer's Hammer* (1977) by Larry Niven and Jerry Pournelle – the story is much the same. Their strength lies in exploring how individuals cope with the situation and the resilience of humanity. *The Torch* (1920; book, 1948) by Jack Bechdolt sees a divided dystopia emerge, whilst *The Hothouse World* (1931; book, 1965) by Fred MacIsaac depicts a frozen Earth with a remnant surviving in a domed city. In

When Worlds Collide (1933) by Edwin Balmer and Philip Wylie, which was very popular in its day, two errant planets enter the solar system. The first destroys the Earth, but a remnant of humanity escape and settle on the second planet. Both *Shiva Descending* (1980) by Gregory Benford and William Rotsler and *The Hammer of God* (1993) by Arthur C. Clarke concentrate on attempts to destroy approaching asteroids, with varying degrees of success.

There are many variations on the theme. In *The Poison Belt* (1913), Arthur Conan Doyle has Earth pass through a toxic realm in space that does not kill humanity but sends everyone to sleep. It is the earliest of the so-called 'cosy' catastrophe novels for which the British became renowned in the 1950s. Another 'cosy', *The Hopkins Manuscript* (1939) by R.C. Sheriff, best known for the play *Journey's End* (1928), has the Moon crash into the Earth with surprisingly mild results. *Land's End* (1988) by Frederik Pohl and Jack Williamson has a comet strip the ozone layer from the Earth's atmosphere, accelerating the greenhouse effect and destroying most life except for those in underwater cities. The young adult novel *Life As We Knew It* (2006) and its sequels, by Susan Beth Pfeffer, describes life on Earth in the cataclysms that follow the Moon being knocked out of its orbit.

Whilst you might survive a plague, the chances of surviving a cosmic collision are far less likely unless one has time to prepare. And who will?

Left Painting by Luděk Marold for 'The Star' by H. G. Wells from the Christmas number of *The Graphic*, 1897.
LON LD46 NPL

Right David A. Hardy's portrayal of an asteroid strike in a heavily populated area, from *Futures* (2004).

Just imagine. The whole Earth knows an asteroid will strike within the next few hours and there is no escape. What would you do in those final moments?

The oldest and best-known account of extreme weather is that of the biblical flood of which the only survivors were Noah and his family. Similar accounts of this deluge appear in such other ancient records as the Akkadian Epic of Atra-Hasis, the Greek legend of Deucalion and the Mesopotamian story of Utnapishtim, all of which suggest some historical major flood in the eastern Mediterranean. This may well tie in with the legend of Atlantis as told by Plato in *Timaeus* (360BC), which records that Atlantis was wracked by earthquakes and floods and sank beneath the waves.

The global flood that covers the Earth in *The Second Deluge* (1912) by Garrett P. Serviss comes from a spiral nebula through which the Earth passes. The scientist who forecast this has naturally built a huge ark whilst others survive by airship or submarine. In *Deluge* (1927) by S. Fowler Wright, the flood is the result of a storm and major subsidence.

Melting ice caps is the threat behind the floods in *Daiyon kampyōki* (1959; trans. as *Inter Ice Age 4*) by Japan's Kōbō Abe, who foresees a new generation of genetically adapted aquatic humans. In *The Drowned World* (1962) by J.G. Ballard, the ice caps are melting due to increased solar radiation creating huge lagoons across Europe and America. John Christopher reversed Ballard's idea so that a reduction in solar radiation led to global freezing, especially in the temperate zones, in *The World in Winter* (1962).

Ballard also wrote *The Wind from Nowhere* (1961). Though this is the least Ballardian of all his books, it is the one where he explores most closely the impact upon society as mega-hurricanes scour the planet. Global warming causes a whole series of hurricanes in *Mother of Storms* (1994) by John Barnes and *Heavy Weather* (1994) by Bruce Sterling.

The phrase 'global warming' linked to 'climate change' had been used since the mid-1950s, particularly following the work of oceanographer Roger Revelle, but it only came into wider awareness

Above Image of a frozen Earth by Warwick Goble from Herbert C. Fyfe's article 'How will the World End', *Pearson's Magazine*, July 1900. This picture was captioned, 'According to Mr H.G. Wells the world will eventually be frozen over.'
P.P.6004.gmq

Above right *Amazing Stories*, January 1929, Frank R. Paul's cover for Marius's 'The Sixth Glacier', where cosmic conditions start a new ice age.
P.P.6383.ccs

Just imagine. Sea levels have risen in the country where you live, and people have retreated to the higher ground – a series of disconnected islands. Power is restored, but how different will it be living in a world of islands?

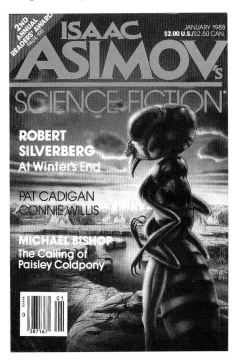

in the mid-1970s following a series of scientific papers. The thriller writer Arthur Herzog was quick to capitalize in *Heat* (1977), where it became a race to convince governments to reverse carbon emissions before the point of no return. Whitley Strieber and James Kunetka also took the thriller route in *Nature's End* (1986), where forty years in the future the Earth's environment can no longer support the excessive population. There is a huge divide between the minority elite and the poor. There are plans to reduce the population on a given day when everyone will be forced to take a tablet, one third of which will be fatal.

George Turner's *The Sea and Summer* (1987; also as *Drowning Towers*) also emphasizes the gap between the rich and the poor. It shows the consequences sixty years hence in an Australia suffering from rising sea levels (Melbourne is mostly underwater) and economic downturn. *Blind Waves* (2000) by Steven Gould shows the fate of the United States when the sea level rises by 100 feet and people are forced to live either on excessively crowded land or in new floating cities, barricaded against illegal immigrants. In *Greenhouse Summer* (1999), Norman Spinrad considers the corporate interests of global warming in the near future, showing how much Earth's future is in the hands of big business and organized crime. Kim Stanley

Robinson also explores the interface between politics and science in trying to overcome the problems of climate change in *Forty Signs of Rain* (2004) and its sequels. In *State of Fear* (2004), however, Michael Crichton decided that global warming had been overrated and that it is all propaganda by eco-terrorists, furthering the cause of environmentalism. The terrorists go so far as to create their own disasters to convince the public.

Although the jury may still be out as regards climate change, most writers are projecting a grim future for the environment unless world governments and corporate interests work together to save the Earth.

Nuclear War

The film *Dr. Strangelove, or How I Learned to Stop Worrying and Love the Bomb* (1964), was based very loosely on Peter George's thriller *Two Hours to Doom* (1958; also as *Red Alert*). Though treated as a black comedy, which George's book was not, the final film scene of Slim Pickens riding the bomb to Earth and the familiar mushroom cloud following the detonation are hauntingly chilling.

The frightening power of nuclear bombs has been only too evident since they exploded over Hiroshima and Nagasaki in 1945, but writers of science fiction had considered this for decades, even before Albert Einstein's famous equation $E=mc^2$ showed the potential of an atomic explosion. Julian Hawthorne had a scientist release atomic energy in 'The Uncertainty About Mr Kippax' (1892), only for him to instantly disintegrate. Robert Cromie went further in *The Crack of Doom* (1895) by having an early experiment destroy an island.

George Griffith had remote-controlled drones with 'radium' bombs, in *The Lord of Labour* (1911), but it was H.G. Wells who first described the use of atomic bombs in a global war in *The World Set Free* (1914). Wells believed atomic bombs would continue to explode over a period of days as the radioactive material decays. The worldwide devastation is so huge that pacifists are able to take control and not only banish all atomic bombs but individual governments as well, bringing in a world state. Though Wells was wide of the mark, he did show how a weapon so powerful would be difficult to use, suggesting an atomic stalemate.

Former British diplomat Harold Nicolson also believed that possession of a nuclear weapon would lead to disarmament in *Public Faces* (1932). It is Britain that develops the bomb but lets it off accidentally in the Caribbean, causing a giant tidal wave that kills thousands and alters the course of the Gulf Stream, changing Europe's climate. It is enough to make other countries lay down their arms – in 1939! In the pages of the science-fiction magazines the writers also looked to a nuclear stalemate (what became the Cold War) notably Robert A. Heinlein in 'Solution Unsatisfactory' (1941).

There was a rush of nuclear war novels in the decade after Hiroshima, of which one of the most original was *Shadow on the Hearth* (1950) by Judith Merril. Rather than look at the big picture Merril focused on a mother and her family and how they cope when America suffers a series of nuclear attacks. Merril showed through the innocence of the mother how rapidly others in positions of authority become corrupt and how soon society is manipulated.

There was the fear that the bomb would fall into the hands of unscrupulous countries or terrorists might gain control, as in Philip Wylie's *The Smuggled Atom Bomb* (1951) and Martin Caidin's *Zoboa* (1986).

More than the other catastrophe themes, nuclear war has lent itself to the post-apocalyptic story. This may be because the chance of a nuclear war seemed more likely than a rogue comet or global flood, which made it more identifiable and marketable. There was no need to write about nuclear war, because that would be over in a short time. It was the aftermath in which everyone was interested.

Many of the early novels were pessimistic. Amongst them are *The Long Loud Silence* (1952) by Wilson Tucker, where the contaminated eastern half of the United States is placed under quarantine; *Level-7* (1959) by Mordecai Roshwald, which follows the depressing fate of the few survivors in underground bunkers after a nuclear war that happened in response to an accident; and *On the Beach* (1957) by British-born Nevil Shute. Shute's book shows how Australia awaits its inevitable fate after all of the Northern Hemisphere has been destroyed and the weather systems gradually bring radiation further south.

Other novels looked at how survivors might cope. In *The Long Tomorrow* (1955)

Right In his article 'How Will the World End' in *Pearson's Magazine*, July 1900, Herbert Fyfe suggested a 'sudden appearance out of the sea of a race of amphibious monsters'. He was years ahead of *Godzilla* or *The Beast from 20,000 Fathoms*!
P.P.6004 gmq

Below The chilling climax of the film *Dr. Strangelove* (1964), directed by Stanley Kubrick.

by Leigh Brackett, survivors turn against science and technology, ban the rebuilding of cities and turn to religion. Walter M. Miller also shows a post-apocalyptic rejection of science and learning as people revert to primitivism in *A Canticle for Leibowitz* (1960). A former engineer establishes a monastery with the sole purpose of preserving learning, just as the monasteries had after the fall of Rome. The book follows the work of the monastery over several centuries as mankind recovers but once again looks to nuclear warfare.

Radioactivity or 'fall-out' was expected to produce mutations, and many post-nuclear stories have looked at monsters or mutants that might arise. This led to the monster movies of the 1950s, of which the best known is *Gojira* (*Godzilla*, 1954), though it started with *The Beast from 20,000 Fathoms* (1953), based on a short story by Ray Bradbury, where atomic tests bring an ancient monster out of hibernation.

By the 1980s research on the effects of nuclear war on climate had given rise to the idea of the 'nuclear winter' – a rapid, catastrophic climate change. Frederik Pohl gave a graphic account of how quickly this would develop in 'Fermi and Frost' (1985), whilst Tatyana Tolstaya gives it the full treatment in a devastated Russia in *Kys* (2000; trans. *The Slynx*, 2003).

The aftermath of a nuclear war is not an easy matter to describe to children and two books stand out in this respect. *Die Letzten Kinder von Schewenborn* (*The Last Children of Schewenborn*, 1983) by Gudrun Pausewang is related by a young boy about his family in the months and years after a nuclear attack, their uncertainties, their struggles and their eventual fate. *When the Wind Blows* (1982) by Raymond Briggs, made into a harrowingly effective animated film in 1986, tells of the final days of an elderly couple as they huddle in their fallout shelter.

To counter the unremitting grimness of most post-apocalyptic fiction, some novels are optimistic about the future of humanity. *Davy* (1964) by Edgar Pangborn is a coming-of-age novel about a teenage orphan who becomes a catalyst for recovery in a world three centuries after the nuclear holocaust, where communities are small, suspicious and technophobic.

Even more positive is *Mecanoscrito del Segundo Origen* (Mecanoscrito, the Second

Source, 1974) by Catalan writer Manuel de Pedrolo. This follows the efforts of two children, one aged fourteen and the other nine, who miraculously survive an alien nuclear holocaust and take on the burden of preserving human culture and keeping life going.

There is much grit and determination in *Damnation Alley* (1969) by Roger Zelazny, which is set in a North America devastated by nuclear fallout and where travel is almost impossible. A prisoner is given the chance of a pardon if he succeeds in a near-suicide mission to take a plague vaccine from Los Angeles to Boston. A similar grim mission is described in *Atomnyi son* (*Nuclear Dream*, 1990) by Sergey Lukyanenko, where an automated missile base is programmed to launch a nuclear strike twenty years after a holocaust. The survivors must find a way to stop it.

In *The Postman* (1985) by David Brin, an opportunist survivor in the years immediately after a war encounters the remains of a postman and his van and decides to deliver his letters. This takes him to small enclaves where he is seen as a sign of hope, bridging the isolation and restoring some sense of continuity.

These novels emphasize that after any catastrophe, hope and determination may be all we have, but it may be enough to start the long road back to salvation.

Above The moment of the nuclear explosion, from Raymond Briggs's When the Wind Blows (1982). YK.1993.b.967

Left The first edition of Walter M. Miller's A Canticle for Leibowitz (1960), with dustjacket by Milton Glaser.

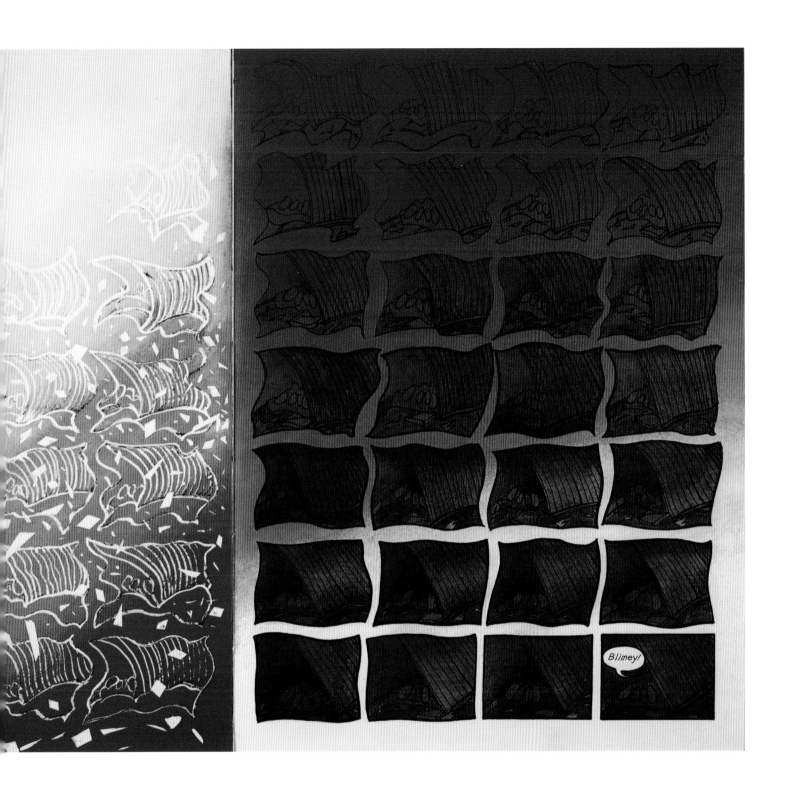

Just imagine. Somehow you have survived
an apocalyptic catastrophe but you can
find no one else alive. How would you survive?
And how would you retain
your sanity and your hope?

The Perfect World?

We have probably all dreamt of a perfect world. That is why there are so many names and descriptions for somewhere we regard as a perfect haven, where all is well, and we can relax and be happy. Paradise is perhaps the most used word and it is one that dates back thousands of years to ancient Persia where it originally meant a walled enclosure or garden. So often paradise is associated with a garden, such as the biblical Garden of Eden or the Greek Elysian Fields. When plans were designed for model new towns in Britain in 1899 they were called Garden Cities, including Letchworth and Welwyn.

Paradise is, eschatologically, where the souls go after death, such as Heaven, Valhalla or the Celtic Tír na nÓg. It is a reward for having lived a good life.

So can a perfect world be attained on Earth? And what is a perfect world? What may seem ideal for you may not be for another. The German philosopher Gottfried Leibniz rationalized that in order to understand good one also had to recognize evil, otherwise there was no comparison. In *Essais de Théodicée sur la bonté de Dieu, la liberté de l'homme et l'origine du mal* (*Theodicy: Essays on the Goodness of God, the Freedom of Man and the Origin of Evil*, 1710), Leibniz argued that it was not possible to have a world without evil, but some worlds may have less evil than others. He contended that as Earth had been made by God, it must be the best of all possible worlds. The French writer Voltaire parodied Leibniz's concept in *Candide* (1759); Candide stumbles across the idyllic city of El Dorado in South America, where the streets are paved with gold and there is no crime or poverty or war.

Writers who first gave thought to an ideal world in fiction were sceptical about achieving it. As far back as 414BC the Greek playwright Aristophanes wrote a satire, *Ornithes* (*The Birds*), in which two Athenians convince the birds to build a city in the sky between Earth and the heavens so that they might converse with the gods on Mount Olympus. This idealized city was called *Nephelokokkygia* or Cloudcuckooland, a word we still use when we mean someone is living a naïve dream.

When Thomas More created his ideal society he called it Utopia, derived from the Greek but with a double meaning: *Eutopia* meaning 'good place' or *Outopia* meaning 'no place'. Samuel Butler called his ideal land Erewhon, an anagram of 'nowhere'.

The opposite of a utopia is a dystopia and, in line with Leibniz's best of all possible worlds, there must also be a worst of all possible worlds. Describing that can highlight what an ideal society has to overcome.

What constitutes a utopia and how it has been explored in fiction is the subject of this section.

Ebenezer Howard's plan of the ideal city from
To-morrow: a peaceful path to real reform (1898).
08275.1.25

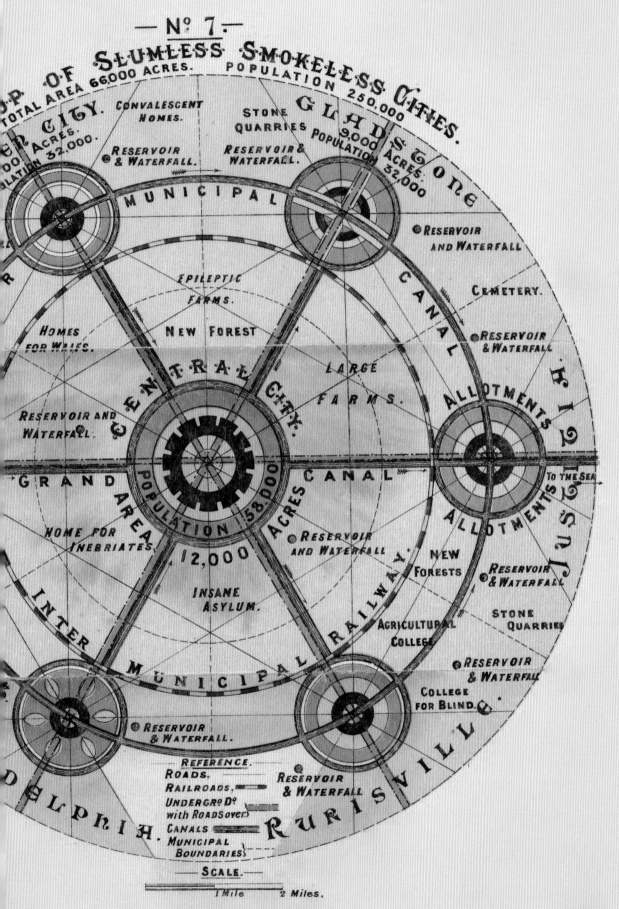

GROUP OF SLUMLESS SMOKELESS CITIES.

TOTAL AREA 66000 ACRES.   POPULATION 250,000

...ER CITY.   CONVALESCENT HOMES.   STONE QUARRIES   GLADSTONE 9,000 ACRES. POPULATION 32,000

...00 ACRES.   RESERVOIR & WATERFALL.   RESERVOIR & WATERFALL.

...LATION 32,000.

MUNICIPAL

RESERVOIR AND WATERFALL

EPILEPTIC FARMS.

CEMETERY.

HOMES FOR WAIFS.   NEW FOREST   RESERVOIR & WATERFALL

CANAL

CENTRAL CITY.   LARGE FARMS.   ALLOTMENTS   HI2...ST

RESERVOIR AND WATERFALL.

GRAND   AREA   POPULATION 58,000   CANAL   TO THE SEA

12,000 ACRES.

HOME FOR INEBRIATES.   RESERVOIR AND WATERFALL   ALLOTMENTS

POPULATION 58,000   NEW FORESTS   RESERVOIR & WATERFALL

12,000

INSANE ASYLUM.   STONE QUARRIES

AGRICULTURAL COLLEGE

INTER   MUNICIPAL   RAILWAY   RESERVOIR & WATERFALL

COLLEGE FOR BLIND.

RESERVOIR & WATERFALL.

...DOLPHIA.   RURISVILLE.

REFERENCE.

ROADS,
RAILROADS,   RESERVOIR & WATERFALL
UNDERGR° D°
with ROADS over)
CANALS
MUNICIPAL BOUNDARIES)

SCALE.

1 Mile   2 Miles.

The First Utopias

12 VTOPIAE INSVLAE TABVLA.

Plato gave much thought to an ideal state in *Politeia* (*The Republic*, 380 BC). He tried to define what constitutes justice and whether a just man is happier than an unjust man. He reasoned that education is at the heart of wisdom, which leads to justice. The work influenced many, not least Sir Thomas More in *Libellus vere aureus, nec minus salutaris quam festivus, de optimo rei publicae statu deque nova insula Utopia* (*A Fruitful and Pleasant Work of the Best State of a Public Weal, and of the New Isle Called Utopia*, 1516).

The story is related by a sailor returned from South America where he discovered the island of Utopia. It has an agrarian economy and socialist outlook – there is no private ownership; everything is held in common. Food is free, there are free hospitals and different religions are tolerated. There is slavery, although slaves are usually condemned criminals or adulterers. Travel is restricted and requires a pass. Utopia is a totalitarian state in common with those in More's day.

In *Utopia*, More comments upon, and sometimes satirizes, opinions of his day. However, it is not always clear when he is being serious. When he suggests that prospective husbands and wives should inspect each other naked before they marry, for example, he may be ridiculing or favouring such openness.

More's work stood on its own for a century, but it left its mark. When Samuel Purchas compiled his books about the world's geography, *Purchas, His Pilgrim* (1613–19), he referred to the Israelites' Promised Land as 'utopian' and the word passed into the language.

There were other utopian writings at this time, such as *Christianopolis* (1619) by Johannes Valentinus Andreae, with its Christian egalitarian society, but it is three other works that brought together utopian ideas with science fiction.

In 1599, the theologian Tommaso Campanella, a friend of Galileo, was tortured by the Inquisition as a heretic and conspirator, and spent twenty-seven years in prison. While there he wrote *Civitas Solis* (*The City of the Sun*), which was eventually published in 1623. A Genoese sea-captain tells of his discoveries in Taprobane, the old name for Sri Lanka, where he is taken to a city high on a hill with seven concentric walls. The city runs on socialist ideals governed by astrological harmonies. Slavery is abolished. Couples may marry if they are astrologically attuned. There is equality in education with an emphasis on science and mechanics. Transport is advanced, with machines that fly by some 'marvellous contrivance'. The people rarely know disease or war and look forward to a world state.

Of particular interest is Francis Bacon's *Nova Atlantis* (*New Atlantis*, 1624). Sailors, lost in the eastern Pacific, find

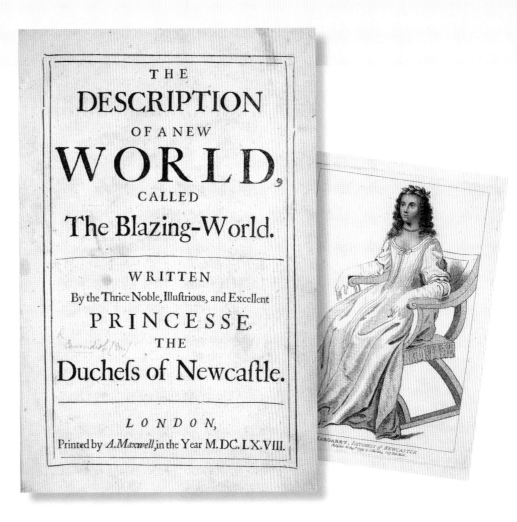

THE
DESCRIPTION
OF A NEW
WORLD,
CALLED
The Blazing-World.

WRITTEN
By the Thrice Noble, Illustrious, and Excellent
PRINCESSE,
THE
Duchefs of Newcaftle.

LONDON,
Printed by *A. Maxwell,* in the Year M.DC.LX.VIII.

the island of Bensalem. They are rebuffed,
but later allowed to land and discover
the island is a technocracy. Its citizens
are directed towards scientific study and
research, co-ordinated by Salomon's
House, which is like a research institute.
Their society includes giant towers,
submarines, flying machines and
something like radio. Bacon laid down
the requirements for a scientifically
enlightened society and his book
encouraged the formation of the 'Invisible
College' in 1645, the forerunner of the
Royal Society.

The Royal Society did not then
admit women, but it did allow Margaret
Cavendish, Duchess of Newcastle, to
attend. An indomitable eccentric, she loved
scientific speculation and appended to her
book *Observations Upon Experimental Philosophy*
(1666) – which itself contains thoughts
on many subjects later explored in science
fiction, such as sub-atomic worlds – the
story 'The Description of a New World,
Called the Blazing World'. A woman
(based on Cavendish) is abducted by a
sea captain to the North Pole where all
but the woman die. The ship passes to

Francis Bacon (1561–1626)
English statesman, philosopher and scientist, Lord Chancellor from 1618–21. When not involved
in state duties Bacon was an inveterate seeker after knowledge, and planned an encyclopaedic
study – *Instauratio Magna*, the 'Great Instauration' – presenting a new approach to philosophy
and science. Bacon started this in 1602 and returned to it at the end of his life. Several volumes
appeared, of which the most significant was *Novum Organum* (New Instrument, 1620), which
remained incomplete. Bacon wanted to make philosophy and science 'more true and more
active', using a new method of reasoning and deduction by which to analyze and understand.
He advocated this approach in his utopian treatise *Nova Atlantis* (1624), believing that through
knowledge mankind would flourish. Bacon's attitude made him both a pioneer scientist and a
godfather of science fiction. He died a dedicated researcher: he is believed to have caught
a chill while testing to see if the cold would help preserve meat, and this developed into
pneumonia.

another planet, on the far side of the Sun,
and the woman is taken to the Emperor,
a handsome young man, who promptly
marries her and allows her to govern the
world. She establishes several scientific
academies to be run by the planet's fish-
men, bird-men, bear-men and similar
species. She also consults the Duchess of
Newcastle (in spirit form) and the two

plan new worlds according to each one's
scientific principles. The book describes
Cavendish's personal utopia, but its
significance is that Cavendish emphasizes
the importance of science in creating
society and determining progress.

Between then, Campanella, Bacon
and Cavendish united the utopia with
science fiction.

At the end of the eighteenth century the American and French revolutions did much to turn minds to new, improved societies. Two utopian works link these countries. *Equality; or a History of Lithconia* (1802; book, 1837) is the earliest American utopia. Attributed to Philadelphian doctor James R. Reynolds, it advocated a communal approach to life and ownership – even marriage is abolished and children are cared for by the community. In *Voyage et aventures de lord William Carisdall en Icarie* (Travel and Adventures of Lord William Carisdall in Icaria, 1840), Étienne Cabet had similar views and proposed the word 'communisme' to describe his system, which attracted the interest of Friedrich Engels and Karl Marx. Cabet had been inspired by both Thomas More and the Welsh philanthropist Robert Owen, who had set up the cotton mill at New Lanark in Scotland along socialist lines in 1816. Cabet took 1,500 followers to the United States to set up a commune in 1848, settling eventually at Nauvoo, Illinois. It was one example of how utopian books inspired followers to create their own societies.

The most influential utopian novel published in America was *Looking Backward, 2000–1887* (1888) by Edward Bellamy. Like Cabet, Bellamy's interest was in social rather than technological change. His character sleeps into the future through hypnotism and awakes in Boston in 2000. All industry has been nationalized. Everyone is gainfully employed and receives the same guaranteed wage, which is paid through a credit-card system. Money no longer exists so there are no banks. People can retire at 45. Food is provided communally. Crime has virtually disappeared, so there are no police, and any rebels are treated as mental patients. There is no war and there is much co-operation between countries to avoid duplication and waste.

The book was a huge success (the third biggest seller of its day after *Uncle Tom's Cabin* and *Ben-Hur*). Bellamy wrote a sequel, *Equality* (1897), which comments that in 2000 people are far less literate because hardly anyone writes any more, women, who have equal rights, wear trousers as the common form of dress, and population levels are controlled. Bellamy is less forthcoming on the status of the black population, but it is assumed they have equality.

The success of *Looking Backward* was measured by more than sales. A host of Bellamy or Nationalist Clubs sprang up across the country (and abroad) to discuss his ideas. There were also several experimental communities established along Bellamy's lines. The book inspired entrepreneur Ebenezer Howard to write *To-morrow: a Peaceful Path to Real Reform* (1898; also as *Garden Cities of To-morrow*) and form the Garden City Association. His plan was to build new, healthy, uncrowded cities, beginning with Letchworth in 1903.

Bellamy's book prompted many sequels, most seeking to attack his ideas. One of the more serious responses was by the British socialist and artist William Morris. He disliked Bellamy's regimented industrialist future, and in *News from Nowhere* (1890) Morris describes a much freer, back-to-basics society that has shunned materialism and technological progress and returned to working closely with Nature. Everything is shared and there are no possessions, not even husbands or wives. People are partners for as long as it feels right. Children are allowed to follow their natural proclivities.

The Austrian Theodor Hertzka, on the other hand, supported Bellamy's views and in *Freiland, ein soziales Zukunftsbild* (Freeland, a social vision of the future, 1890), set in Kenya, he demonstrated how capitalism and a free economy was the way to prosperity.

Morris's future may seem too hedonistic to work, Bellamy's too prescriptive and Hertzka's too risky. But all were serious manifestos for an idealized future.

Cover of first British edition of Edward Bellamy's *Looking Backward 2000–1887* (1889). 1509/4173

Frontispiece from the Kelmscott Press 1892 edition of *News from Nowhere* by William Morris. C.43.e.9

Edward Bellamy (1850–98)

American attorney-turned-newspaperman, remembered as a social theorist and for his book *Looking Backward*. Bellamy's utopian novel was so popular, selling over a million copies, that it overshadowed his other work, including some other science fiction. He found fame with *Dr Heidenhoff's Process* (1880), spoiled by the 'it was all a dream' revelation but interesting for exploring the idea of removing unwanted memories to ensure happiness. In 'The Blindman's World' (1886), an astronomer falls asleep at his telescope; his spirit visits Mars and learns that the Martians have foreknowledge, yet this does not affect their lives. 'To Whom This May Come' (1888) is set on a remote island whose inhabitants are telepathic, which means no one has any secrets. These three stories each explore different human concerns (unwanted memory, predestination, secrecy) that might otherwise affect happiness. Bellamy wrote one further piece about future Boston, 'Woman in the Year 2000', where he questioned whether equality meant women were more likely to marry for love rather than wealth!

Margaret Cavendish aside, most early utopias were social experiments written by men. Reassuringly, women were usually treated as equals, though there is a sense in some books that this is done rather patronisingly. Bellamy's hero, Julian West, is alarmed when he discovers the extent of female equality, and is shocked when his fiancée reveals she normally wears trousers.

So when women turned to writing utopias it was to express their own freedoms. The first American utopia written by a woman was 'Three Hundred Years Hence' (in *Camperdown*, 1836) by Mary Griffith. A man dreams of the future in 2135 when there has been extensive urbanization of the countryside, automation in the cities and a new transport network. A new means of propulsion was invented by a woman. Women are regarded as equals and play a full part in society. Horses and dogs are almost extinct. Slavery has been abolished and all former slaves were rehabilitated to Liberia and other colonies of their choosing. However, the American Indian has died out.

Mary Bradley Lane, writing as Princess Zarovitch, went much further in *Mizora* (1881; book, 1890). The Princess is shipwrecked near the North Pole and carried into the hollow Earth where she finds the land of Mizora occupied only by women. Following the discovery of parthenogenesis, men became extinct and only female babies are created. The land is scientifically advanced with aeroplanes and electric vehicles. All food is synthetic except for certain fruits. There is no religion. The inhabitants are fascinated by the Princess and want to know of her experience of men. The Princess believes that all evil originates from men, without whom there would be no crime.

There is a similar isolated all-female community in *Herland* (1915; book, 1979) by Charlotte Perkins Gilman. Women are again born parthenogenetically, but, to ensure the strain does not weaken, men

---

Katharine Burdekin (1896–1963)
British writer, whose later novels appeared under the pseudonym Murray Constantine – her authorship was not discovered until 1985. Under her own name she wrote some early time travel fantasies, including *The Rebel Passion* (1929) where a twelfth-century monk has a vision of the twenty-first century reverting to a medieval state after an apocalyptic war, but a world where women are equal and anyone abnormal is sterilized. She adopted the Constantine alias for fear of repercussions because of the subject-matter of her disturbing novel *Swastika Night* (1937). It is set seven centuries after World War II, which Hitler won alongside the Japanese. The world, with its 'cult of masculinity', is divided between these two super powers. History has been rewritten. All Jews have been exterminated and women are kept in concentration camps and used only for breeding. After Burdekin's death several unpublished manuscripts were found, including *The End of This Day's Business* (1989). Set in the year 6250, women are firmly in control and men are subordinate and conditioned to accept their inferiority. Women have created a world of peace and beauty, but one woman questions why a matriarchy should be any more acceptable than a patriarchy, and initiates steps towards a dignified and humane egalitarian world.

---

are occasionally allowed in for mating. Three men find their way into the remote valley of Herland, one of whom relates the story. He is amazed to find a society run efficiently by women, especially one so technologically advanced. Each man has rather stereotypical views of women. One finds it difficult to explain love as distinct from sex to a woman and is accused of rape.

Elizabeth Burgoyne Corbett set a utopia in Ireland in *New Amazonia* (1889). Conflict between Britain and Ireland resulted in the Irish population being almost wiped out. The British government replaced it with surplus women who, by the year 2472, run society. Men, who represent bigotry, corruption and immorality, have been sidelined, and women use various techniques to sustain bodily perfection, including eradicating malformed children. They have increased their life span and grown considerably in height.

The Bengali social reformer Roquia Sakhawat Hussain wrote 'The Sultana's Dream', published in India in 1905. A woman dreams of a future where women are in charge and men are excluded, a reversal of the practice of purdah. Women had overcome men

through the use of their brain power and the technologically advanced future was down to their ingenuity.

The prospect of female supremacy was not necessarily appreciated by the Victorian male, particularly with the rise of suffragism in Britain, highlighting that what is one group's utopia is another's dystopia. In *The Revolt of Man* (1882), Walter Besant looked at a future Britain where women were in charge and men had been disenfranchised with no legal rights. It was a complete role reversal. Scientific and political progress has ceased. Women marry whom they choose and the man has no say. If he refuses he can be imprisoned. Eventually the men revolt and the old order is restored.

The 1970s saw a significant increase in the depiction of feminist societies, of which two key works stand out. Joanna Russ's *The Female Man* (1975) is set in four parallel worlds, each with a different manifestation of the same woman. One is contemporary with the novel, one is in the recent misogynistic past, and two are alternate futures. One is an all-female utopia 800 years in the future after men have been wiped out, it is believed by a plague. The other is a segregated future where men and women have separated

In *Anno Domini 2000* (1889), by
the New Zealand politician Sir Julius
Vogel, women hold many powerful
political offices including President of
the United States.

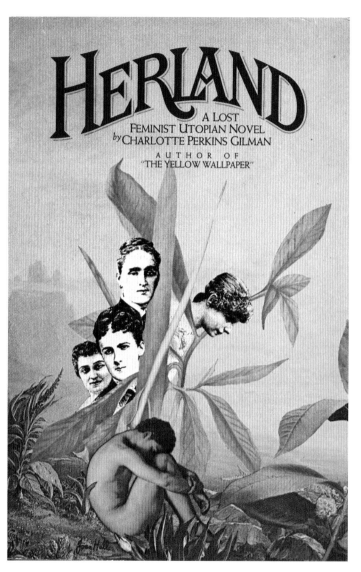

Herland by Charlotte Perkins Gilman,
the first book publication in 1979,
sixty-four years after the novel was
originally written.

Image from the film *The Handmaid's Tale* (1990), directed by Volker Schlöndorff, based on the novel by Margaret Atwood.

and are in conflict. Russ compares each society through each woman's viewpoint and reveals how the all-female utopia really came about. Called Whileaway, it is primarily agrarian but has developed genetic engineering to allow procreation.

Marge Piercy's *Woman on the Edge of Time* (1976) has some similarities. The eponymous 'woman', Consuelo, is a mental patient who is contacted by a woman from the future and learns that her actions will generate either a future utopia or dystopia. The utopia is an agrarian communal society where bigotry, pollution and totalitarianism have been eliminated. The dystopia has the population herded like cattle purely for their organs or for the sexual gratification of a wealthy elite.

Perhaps the best-known recent dystopian novel by a woman is *The Handmaid's Tale* (1985) by Margaret Atwood. It is set a few decades hence when the government of the United States has been overthrown and a totalitarian state has emerged – militaristic, racist and chauvinistic. Women are segregated and have no authority. They are divided into various classes, one of which is handmaids, the equivalent of concubines. All African-Americans and Jews have been 'removed', believed exterminated. Abortions are illegal, but any deformed babies are eradicated. Atwood may well have described the worst of all possible worlds, which is all the more chilling because for those in power, it is a utopia.

Just imagine. What criteria would you use as the basis of a perfect world? How might these differ from those of your friends and family? How would you reconcile any differences amicably?

Freedom or Oppression?

The two best-known anti-utopias of the twentieth century are *Brave New World* (1932) by Aldous Huxley and *Nineteen Eighty-Four* (1949) by George Orwell. Despite often being bracketed together they have little in common. *Brave New World* is really a parody of works that saw the advantage of a World State, notably H.G. Wells's *A Modern Utopia* (1905). Wells believed that the only way the world would see peace would be through a world-governing body. In *A Modern Utopia*, which is more a treatise than a novel, he shows how scientific progress will allow a global infrastructure for transport, agriculture and commerce that should balance inequalities. He also saw the importance of global standards in education and gender equality. His ideas are in direct descent from Bacon's *New Atlantis*.

Huxley, however, could only see a World State taking the lowest common denominator, which would be dictated by the excesses of the United States and other powerful nations. The end result is a world where everyone exercises apparent freedom (such as legalized drugs, recreational sex, no family ties), but where they are in fact rigidly controlled by the State from before birth. Embryos are chemically manipulated to produce the right children. *Brave New World* is a clever portrayal of a superficial utopia that is an insidious dystopia.

Nineteen Eighty-Four is a self-evident dystopia from the start. Set in one of three global totalitarian super-states, where the population is constantly monitored by 'Big Brother', the Thought Police, everyone must obey a strict set of codes. Even thinking outside these codes is punishable. The main character, Winston Smith, works for the state doctoring photographs and generally revising the historical record. Love is forbidden and when Smith falls in love he is punished, forced to betray his lover and brainwashed so that once again he loves Big Brother. Orwell's vision is so indelible that it has passed into the national psyche; we still use '1984' to mean an

The dustjacket of the first edition of
Brave New World by Aldous Huxley
(1932). Design by Leslie Holland.

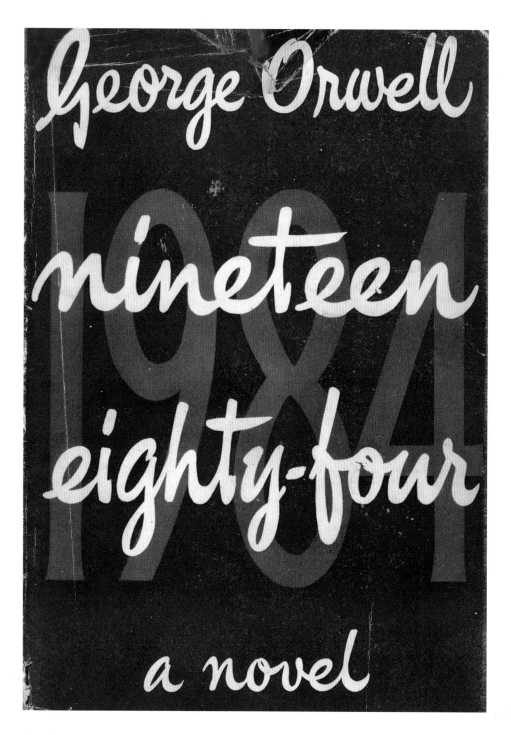

publish it and it was officially banned by the Soviet Union after an abridged version was serialized in 1927. The full version was not published there until 1988. It was published in the USA in English in 1924 without Zamyatin's permission and the first full Russian version was published in the USA in 1952.

The dystopia can be traced back at least as far as Émile Souvestre's *Le monde tel qu'il sera* (The World as it Will Be, 1846), which foresaw how commercialism would make humanity a slave to the machine and thereby to its corporate or government masters. Ignatius Donnelly similarly foresaw in *Caesar's Column* (1890) how state control could easily fall into the hands of ruthless, corrupt individuals. Jack London took this further in *The Iron Heel* (1907), where a capitalist oligarchy seeks to gain absolute power in America but is defeated by the socialists – both sides using similar techniques – and a form of socialist utopia prevails. Jerome K. Jerome lampooned utopian ideals with powerful effect in 'A New Utopia' (1891), where equality is taken to the inevitable extreme resulting in unbending regimentation. Kurt Vonnegut did the same in 'Harrison Bergeron' (1961), where any signs of perfection in people are handicapped so as to maintain a sense of equality.

What dystopias alert us to is that for a society to feel like a utopia to its citizens there must be choice, and it must be progressive, with the hope of good times ahead. That mood prevailed in several stories and novels that appeared in China at the start of the twentieth century in the years of 'modernization' shortly after the Boxer Rebellion fighting against Western imperialism. The political reformer Liang Qichao did not finish his novel *Xin Zhongguo weilai ji* (The Future of New China, 1902), which mapped out a prosperous China on the world stage in 1960. Nevertheless, what he completed inspired others. In *Xin Zhongguo* (New China, 1910), Lu Shi'e depicted a China that is so prosperous it has a surfeit of wealth and thus builds a powerful new state. Most significant is *Xin jiyuan* (New Era, 1908) by Biheguan Zhuren, set in 1999, where China has a democratic, constitutional monarchy and is technologically advanced. It develops

oppressive totalitarian regime, even though the date is now decades in the past.

Orwell's novel was inspired by Yevgenii Zamyatin's *My* (*We*). Set several centuries in the future after the Two Hundred Years' War has wiped out most of humanity, it takes place in a highly regimented city-state encircled by the 'Green Wall', which is supposed to keep out the post-apocalyptic world. Everything in the future is state controlled, including when you eat and when you can have sex.

No one is allowed to think for themselves or be creative. People are known only by numbers. D-503 falls in love with the subversive I-330, who is planning to take over a new spaceship that D has helped design. D does not report her, but the authorities discover the plan from D's diaries. He is arrested and subjected to the 'Great Operation' (like a lobotomy), after which he is able to watch I's torture and execution without concern. Written in 1920, Russian publishers refused to

new weapons to wage a world war and establish a global Chinese utopian empire.

Ivan Yefremov was the writer who revived science fiction in Russia after the Stalinist era. In *Tumannost' Andromedy* (trans. as *Andromeda*, 1957), he depicted an idyllic Earth in the year 3000 with a society built on humanistic Marxist principles and with technological marvels. It is the only convincing communist utopia, but even Yefremov had second thoughts. The sequel *Chas Byka* (*The Hour of the Bull*, 1968; book, 1970), set two centuries later, compared the ideal communist state with a dictatorship on another planet. Yefremov disguised the dictatorship as based on the Chinese model of communism, but many interpreted it as criticizing the Soviet Union. The book edition had already been heavily censored but all copies were withdrawn, and it was not republished in Russia until 1988.

All these utopias and dystopias require strong nations that can act with authority on the world stage, and have total control over their citizens. Achieving this requires not only social reform, including education akin to indoctrination, but also technological advance to allow global surveillance.

The line between utopia and dystopia is clearly in the eye of the beholder, whether that be the individual or the state. Neither provides a clear-cut answer as to what constitutes a perfect world.

In *The Stepford Wives* (1972), by Ira Levin, a new resident of the idyllic town of Stepford, Connecticut, is puzzled by the submissiveness of the wives to their husbands and how they go about their daily routine in almost robotic servitude. She discovers to her horror that the women have indeed been converted into automatons, responding to their husbands' every whim. For the husbands this may seem like the perfect world, but what about the women?

No matter what steps are made to try and make the perfect society, the one problem is people. No one would agree on what makes the perfect world unless it was full of like-minded clones or automatons, and what kind of world is that?

What is more, the idea of adapting people, whether through selective breeding, genetic engineering or what is generally called eugenics, seems abhorrent because linked with developing the perfect human is eradicating the imperfect. The science of eugenics was popularized by Francis Galton in *Inquiries into Human Faculties* (1883). Soon after, the American educator Edward Payson Jackson completed *A Demigod* (1886) about the selective breeding of a superman from a programme first developed in Greece by a far-thinking doctor two centuries before. The latest offspring of this programme, Hector, is a man of incredible beauty, strength, intellect and agility, with *Matrix*-like abilities to dodge bullets. He is, in effect, the first superhero.

The basic problem with eugenics is who defines perfection and what happens to those who don't fit? In S. Fowler Wright's 'P.N. 40' (1929) – the title refers to an individual in a future when everyone is known by numbers – a woman is designated as a suitable wife but refuses to marry and escapes the country with another. The child in *Gladiator* (1930) by Philip Wylie is the result of his mother having been fed a new serum that conveys strength. The child, Hugo, turns out to be immensely strong, seems to be impervious to harm and is very athletic – his giant leaps are almost like flying. Yet Hugo is not happy and spends much of his life trying to hide, until at last he comes to terms with his abilities and decides to raise a new race of super-humans. Fate intervenes and he is struck by lightning, implying man should not vie with God in creating a master race.

Most stories of beings with enhanced 'super' abilities tend to consider them as troubled individuals who may be the next step in evolution but are either hunted or go into hiding, as in A.E. van Vogt's

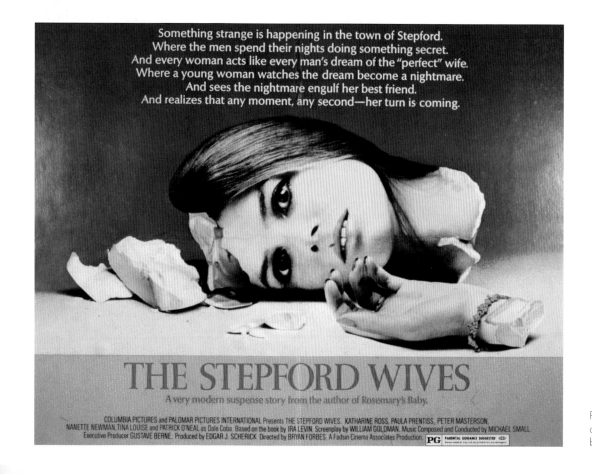

Poster for the 1975 film adaptation of *The Stepford Wives*, directed by Bryan Forbes.

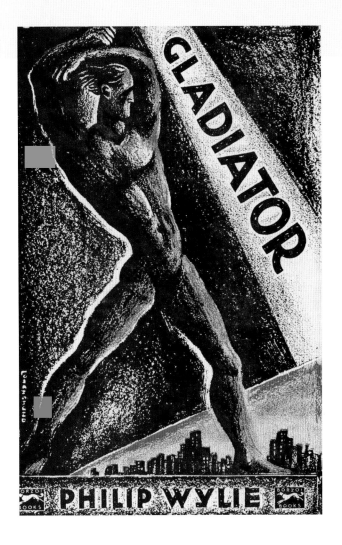

Slan (1940; book, 1946) or Wilmar Shiras's *Children of the Atom* (1953).

Arthur C. Clarke's *Childhood's End* (1953) shows that perfection cannot be achieved by humans alone. As Earth enters the Space Age it is visited by aliens who become known as the Overlords and help Earth's nations enter an age of prosperity. They are benign even though they later reveal themselves to be in the form of our image of demons. After fifty years newly born children show they have psychic powers and the Overlords reveal they are preparing humans for a merger with the Overmind, a cosmic intelligence that will take humans onto the next stage of evolution. Clarke's utopia, though, is not a human utopia on Earth. How can that possibly be achieved while humans still have all their faults and frailties?

The film *It's a Wonderful Life* (1946) is based on a short fantasy, 'The Greatest Gift' (1943) by Philip Van Doren Stern.

A man wishes he had never been born and his guardian angel shows him what the world would have been like without him. It brings into focus all the good he has done in his life. If all that good were part of a genuine altruistic community rather than just an individual, might that lead to a perfect world?

There is one book where the portrayal of an altruistic community is so memorable that its name has passed into the language – Shangri-La. In *Lost Horizon* (1933), James Hilton describes life in a remote Himalayan monastery, in the secluded Valley of the Blue Moon that has life-prolonging qualities. The High Lama has arranged that the monastery will preserve the treasures of the world from what might be the next ultimate war. Hidden from all that chaos, Shangri-La is the perfect haven and the salvation of the world.

Perhaps we must all hope for our Shangri-La.

Chronology

This presents in chronological order a selection of the more significant books and events to show the evolution of science fiction covered in this book.

414 BC   Aristophanes, *Nephelokokkygia*
380 BC   Plato, *Politeia*

c170   Lucian of Samosata, *True History* and *Icaromenippus*

1298–9   Marco Polo relates *Livres des merveilles du monde*

1370   Jean de Mandeville, *Travels*

1516   Thomas More, *Utopia*
1522   First circumnavigation of the Earth
1543   Nicolaus Copernicus, *De revolutionibus orbium coelestium*

1609   Johannes Kepler completes *Somnium*
1610   Galileo, *Sidereus Nuncius* reveals the Moon as a distinct world
1623   Tommaso Campanella, *Civitas Solis*
1624   Francis Bacon, *Nova Atlantis*
1628   Francis Godwin completes *The Man in the Moone*, the first work of science fiction written in English
1638   John Wilkins, *The Discovery of a World in the Moone*
1650   Cyrano de Bergerac completes *L'Autre Monde ou les États et Empires de la Lune* and *Les États et Empires du Soleil* introducing the idea of rocket-powered travel
1666   Margaret Cavendish, 'The Description of a New World, Called the Blazing World'
1686   Bernard de Fontenelle, *Entretiens sur la Pluralité des Mondes*

1726   Jonathan Swift, *Gulliver's Travels*
1733   Samuel Madden, *Memoirs of the Twentieth Century*, first to consider a future world
1741   Ludvig Holberg, *Niels Klims underjordiske Reise*
1751   Robert Paltock's *The Life and Adventures of Peter Wilkins* introduced the lost-race theme
1752   Voltaire, *Micromegas* with the first visit to Earth by a being from another star
1771   Louis-Sébastien Mercier, *L'an deux mille quatre cent quarante*, portrays a transformed future
1775   Louis Guillaume de la Folie's *Le Philosophe sans pretention, ou l'homme rare* introduces the idea of an electric-powered flying machine
1781   William Herschel discovered Uranus, the first 'new' planet; Johan Wessel *Anno 7603* depicts a feminist future
1785   Rudolf Raspe, *Baron Münchhausen's Narrative of his Marvellous Travels*

1802   Rétif de la Bretonne, *Les Posthumes*, the first to chart a future history
1805   Cousin de Grainville, *The Last Man*
1810   Julius von Voss, *Ini*, depicts a united Europe
1815   Edward Burney's 'Q.Q. Esq.'s Journey to the Moon' with the first depiction of a space suit
1816   E.T.A. Hoffmann's 'Der Sandman' describes a realistic humanoid automaton
1818   Mary Shelley's *Frankenstein*, considered by some the world's first novel of science fiction

1825   William Heath produces a series of posters on 'The March of Intellect'
1826   Mary W. Shelley, *The Last Man*, the first science-fiction disaster novel
1827   Joseph Atterley, *A Voyage to the Moon* introduces anti-gravity; Jane Webb, *The Mummy*
1832   Charles Babbage demonstrates his Difference Engine, the first automatic calculator
1835   Richard Adams Locke's Moon Hoax; Edgar Allan Poe, 'Hans Phaal'
1836   Louis-Napoléon Geoffroy-Château, *Napoléon et la conquête du monde*, the first detailed uchronia; Mary Griffith, 'Three Hundred Years Hence', first American utopia by a woman
1838   Edgar Allan Poe, *The Narrative of Arthur Gordon Pym of Nantucket*; S. Austin, Jr., 'The Comet' has a comet destroy life on Earth
1840   Étienne Cabet, *Voyage et aventures de lord William Carisdall en Icarie* coins the word 'communisme'
1842   Alfred Lord Tennyson, 'Locksley Hall' foresees a world government
1846   Émile Souvestre, *Le Monde tel qu'il sera*, one of the earliest dystopias
1847   John L. Riddell, *Orrin Lindsay's Plan of Aerial Navigation*, the first 'hard' science-fiction story and the first to depict a lifeless Moon
1851   First use of phrase 'science fiction' in William Wilson's *A Little Earnest Book Upon a Great Old Subject*
1854   C.I. Defontenay, *Star ou Psi de Cassiopée*, the first to depict an extended alien society
1859   Charles Darwin, *On the Origin of Species*
1864   Jules Verne, *Voyage au centre de la Terre*
1865   Jules Verne, *De La Terre à la Lune*; Achille Eyraud, *Voyage à Venus* with the first journey to Venus
1869   Edward Everett Hale, 'The Brick Moon', describing the first manned artificial satellite
1871   George Chesney's 'The Battle of Dorking', establishes fear of invasion in Britain; Edward Bulwer Lytton, *The Coming Race*
1872   Camille Flammarion's 'Lumen' considers the consequences of faster-than-light travel
1870   Jules Verne, *Vingt mille lieues sous les mers*
1872   Samuel Butler, *Erewhon*, raises the idea of machine evolution
1876   Thomas Edison establishes research laboratory at Menlo Park
1877   Giovanni Schiaparelli reports seeing *canali* on Mars
1879   Edward Page Mitchell's 'The Ablest Man in the World', describes the first 'cyborg'
1880   Percy Greg's *Across the Zodiac*, coins the word 'astronaut'; William DeLisle Hay, *The Doom of the Great City* describes London's death from pollution
1881   Edward Page Mitchell, 'The Clock That Went Backward', uses a device to travel through time; Mary Bradley Lane, *Mizora*
1882   Walter Besant, *The Revolt of Man*
1883   Albert Robida's *Le Vingtième siècle* illustrates the future of 1952
1884   Edwin A. Abbott, *Flatland*, the first to describe a two-dimensional world
1885   Richard Jefferies, *After London*, the first eco-catastrophe novel
1886   Edward Payson Jackson, *A Demigod*, describes the first superhero

1887   Gaspar y Rimbau, 'El Anacronópete', the first to create a time machine
1888   Edward Bellamy, *Looking Backward, 2000–1887*
1889   Frank R. Stockton, *The Great War Syndicate*, describes a capitalist war; John Ames Mitchell, *The Last American*; Sir Julius Vogel, *Anno Domini 2000* has female President of the USA
1890   Ignatius Donnelly, *Caesar's Column* depicts New York as a mega-city; William Morris, *News from Nowhere*, an anti-industrialist utopia
1891   Jerome K. Jerome, 'A New Utopia'
1893   George Griffith, *The Angel of the Revolution*; H.G. Wells, 'The Man of the Year Million'
1894   William Le Queux, *The Great War in England in 1897*
1895   H.G. Wells, *The Time Machine*; Robert Cromie, *The Crack of Doom*, foresees atomic energy
1896   H.G. Wells, *The Island of Dr. Moreau*; Konstantin Tsiolkovsky begins *Vne Zemli*, with its development of a space colonization programme.
1897   H.G. Wells, *The War of the Worlds*, the first hostile alien invasion, in *Pearson's Magazine*; Kurd Lasswitz, *Auf Zwei Planeten*, describes the first fixed orbiting space station; George Griffith's 'The Great Crellin Comet' has a giant gun divert the path of a comet
1898   M.P. Shiel, *The Yellow Danger*
1899   H.G. Wells, *When the Sleeper Wakes*

1900   Robert W. Cole, *The Struggle for Empire*, the first to depict rival stellar empires
1901   H.G. Wells, *The First Men in the Moon*; M. P. Shiel, *The Purple Cloud*; L. Frank Baum describes a video-recorder in *The Master Key*
1902   Albert Robida, *L'horloge des siècles*, the first novel of time in reverse; Jerzy Żuławski, *Na Srebrnym Globie* with its harsh portrayal of a moon landing
1904   August Niemann's *Der Weltkrieg – Deutsche Träume* depicts a World War
1905   Albert Einstein's Theory of Special Relativity; H.G. Wells, *A Modern Utopia*; Rudyard Kipling, 'With the Night Mail'; Roquia Sakhawat Hussain, 'The Sultana's Dream'
1906   William Le Queux, *The Invasion of 1910*
1907   Rudolf Martin's *Berlin-Bagdad* depicts German control of the skies; Jack London, *The Iron Heel*
1908   H.G. Wells, *The War in the Air* foresees the end of civilization; Biheguan Zhuren, *Xin jiyuan* describes a global Chinese utopian empire
1909   E.M. Forster, 'The Machine Stops' depicts world reliant on technology; mobile phone predicted in anonymous 'A Glimpse into the Future'
1911   Hugo Gernsback begins 'Ralph 124C 41+'
1912   Edgar Rice Burroughs, 'Under the Moons of Mars'; Arthur Conan Doyle, *The Lost World*; William Hope Hodgson, *The Night Land*; Garrett P. Serviss, *The Second Deluge*
1913   Arthur Conan Doyle, *The Poison Belt*
1914   Jack London, *The Scarlet Plague*; Arthur Conan Doyle's 'Danger!' suggests the submarine blockade of Britain; H.G. Wells, *The World Set Free* foresees atomic warfare

1915 Charlotte Perkins Gilman, 'Herland'
1916 Frigyes Karinthy, *Utazás Faremidóba* depicts a world of intelligent machines; Cleveland Moffett, *The Conquest of America*
1917 Perley Poore Sheehan and Robert H. Davis's play *Blood and Iron* depicts cyborg soldiers
1919 Francis Stevens, *The Heads of Cerberus*, depicts alternate futures
1920 Yevgenii Zamyatin writes *We*
1921 Karel Čapek's *Rossum's Universal Robots* first produced
1923 Alexei Tolstoi, *Aelita*; H.G. Wells, *Men Like Gods*; J.J. Connington, *Nordenholt's Millions*
1926 *Amazing Stories*, the first all science-fiction magazine appears (April)
1927 Fritz Lang's film *Metropolis*; J.W. Dunne's *An Experiment with Time* proposes that all time exists at once; S. Fowler Wright, *Deluge*
1928 E.E. Smith, 'The Skylark of Space' brings space opera to the science-fiction magazines
1929 Fritz Lang's film *Frau im Mond*; Hugo Gernsback coins phrase 'science fiction' in the form we now understand it
1930 Olaf Stapledon's *Last and First Men* creates a vast future history; Laurence Manning and Fletcher Pratt's 'City of the Living Dead' describes humans reliant on virtual reality; Miles J. Breuer's 'The Fitzgerald Contraction' considers time dilation in space travel; Philip Wylie, *Gladiator*, the book that inspired the creation of Superman
1931 John W. Campbell, Jr., 'Islands of Space' suggests concept of hyperspace
1932 Aldous Huxley, *Brave New World*
1933 Maurice Renard's *Le maître de la lumière* suggests a glass that slows down time; James Hilton, *Lost Horizon* set in Shangri-La; Nathan Schachner, 'Ancestral Voices', explores the 'grandfather paradox'; Edwin Balmer and Philip Wylie, *When Worlds Collide*
1934 Stanley G. Weinbaum's 'A Martian Odyssey' depicts alien societies
1937 Olaf Stapledon, *Star Maker*; Murray Constantine, *Swastika Night*
1938 Jack Williamson's 'The Legion of Time', introduces the 'Jonbar Point' concept; first appearance of Superman in *Action Comics* (June); Orson Welles's radio production of *The War of the Worlds* causes panic
1939 Eric Frank Russell, *Sinister Barrier* in *Unknown*
1940 Don Wilcox's 'The Voyage That Lasted 600 Years' introduces idea of generation starship; A.E. van Vogt, 'Slan' serialized
1941 Isaac Asimov develops the Three Laws of Robotics; Robert A. Heinlein, 'By His Bootstraps'
1942 Isaac Asimov's 'Foundation', first story in the Foundation series; Jack Williamson's 'Collision Orbit' suggested terraforming
1945 Murray Leinster's 'First Contact' considers how human-aliens communicate; Arthur C. Clarke's 'Extra-Terrestrial Relays' proposes global communication via geostationary satellites
1946 Murray Leinster's 'A Logic Named Joe' predicts home computers and the internet

1947 Jack Williamson, 'With Folded Hands...', the first part of *The Humanoids* appears in *Astounding SF*; Ward Moore, *Greener Than You Think* shows bioengineering causing chaos
1948 Peter Phillips's 'Dreams Are Sacred', perhaps the earliest use of entering virtual reality
1949 George Orwell, *Nineteen Eighty-Four*; George R. Stewart, *Earth Abides*
1950 Ray Bradbury, *The Martian Chronicles*
1951 Robert A. Heinlein, *The Puppet Masters*; John Wyndham, *The Day of the Triffids*
1952 Ray Bradbury, 'A Sound of Thunder'; James Blish coins 'pantropy' in 'Surface Tension'
1953 Arthur C. Clarke, *Childhood's End*; Ward Moore, *Bring the Jubilee*; Alfred Bester, *The Demolished Man*; John Wyndham, *The Kraken Wakes*
1954 Hal Clement, *Mission of Gravity*, depicting a truly alien environment; Jack Finney, *The Body Snatchers*; Isaac Asimov, *The Caves of Steel*; Fredric Brown's 'Answer' foresees the technological singularity
1955 John Wyndham, *The Chrysalids*
1956 Arthur C. Clarke, *The City and the Stars*; John Christopher, *The Death of Grass*
1957 John Wyndham, *The Midwich Cuckoos*; Nevil Shute, *On the Beach*; Ivan Yefremov, *Tumannost' Andromedy*
1959 Robert A. Heinlein, *Starship Troopers* and 'All You Zombies'; Philip K. Dick, *Time Out of Joint*
1960 J.G. Ballard's 'The Voices of Time' appears in *New Worlds*; Walter M. Miller, Jr., *A Canticle for Leibowitz*; Harry Harrison, *Deathworld*
1961 Stanisław Lem, *Solaris*
1962 Naomi Mitchison, *Memoirs of a Spacewoman*; Philip K. Dick, *The Man in the High Castle*; J.G. Ballard, *The Drowned World*
1963 Iron Man cyborg superhero in *Tales of Suspense* (March); Frank Herbert's 'Dune World', the start of his Dune series, begins in *Analog*; *Dr Who* TV series begins (23 November);
1964 J.G. Ballard's 'The Terminal Beach' appears in *New Worlds* plus novel *The Burning World*; Daniel F. Galouye's *Simulacron-3* describes a virtual world; Philip K. Dick, *The Three Stigmata of Palmer Eldritch* challenges concepts of reality; Stanisław Lem, *Bajki robotów*; John Brunner, *The Whole Man*; Stanley Kubrick's film *Dr. Strangelove*
1965 Arthur C. Clarke's 'Dial F for Frankenstein' sows seed for the internet
1966 Harry Harrison's *Make Room! Make Room!*, the basis of the film *Soylent Green*; *Star Trek* TV series begins (8 September); Richard Fleischer's film *Fantastic Voyage*
1967 Philip E. High, *These Savage Futurians* foresees nanotechnology
1968 Stanley Kubrick's film, *2001: A Space Odyssey*; Philip K. Dick, *Do Androids Dream of Electric Sheep?*; John Brunner, *Stand on Zanzibar*
1969 Ursula K. Le Guin's *The Left Hand of Darkness*; Kurt Vonnegut, *Slaughterhouse-Five*; Michael Moorcock, *Behold the Man*
1970 Ivan Yefremov, *Chas Byka*; Larry Niven, *Ringworld*
1971 Michael Moorcock, *The Warlord of the Air*, one of the earliest 'steampunk' novels; Robert Silverberg, *The World Inside*

1972 Isaac Asimov, *The Gods Themselves*; Martin Caidin, *Cyborg*; John Brunner, *The Sheep Look Up*, the classic novel of pollution
1974 Joe Haldeman, *The Forever War*; Ursula K. Le Guin, *The Dispossessed*; Manuel de Pedrolo, *Mecanoscrito del Segundo Origen*
1975 John Brunner's *The Shockwave Rider* foresees computer viruses; Robert Anton Wilson and Robert Shea's *Illuminatus!* trilogy; Samuel R. Delany, *Dhalgren*; Joanna Russ, *The Female Man*
1976 Marge Piercy, *Woman on the Edge of Time*; James Tiptree, Jr., '"Houston, Houston, Do You Read?"'
1977 George Lucas's film *Star Wars* and Steven Spielberg's film, *Close Encounters of the Third Kind* released; Larry Niven and Jerry Pournelle, *Lucifer's Hammer*; Frederik Pohl, *Gateway*
1979 Doris Lessing's *Shikasta*; Ridley Scott's film, *Alien*
1981 Vernor Vinge's *True Names* describes avatars and cyber-manipulation
1982 William Gibson coins 'cyberspace' in 'Burning Chrome'; Bruce Sterling begins Shaper series with 'Spider Rose'; Raymond Briggs, *When the Wind Blows*; Steven Spielberg's film, *E.T.* and Ridley Scott's film *Blade Runner*
1983 Bruce Bethke coins 'cyberpunk'; Gudrun Pausewang, *Die Letzten Kinder von Schewenborn*
1984 William Gibson, *Neuromancer*, the first major cyberpunk novel; Vernor Vinge, *The Peace War*
1985 Greg Bear, *Blood Music* foresees 'grey goo' hypothesis of destruction by nanotechnology; Frederik Pohl, 'Fermi and Frost' portrays a nuclear winter; David Brin, *The Postman*; Margaret Atwood, *The Handmaid's Tale*
1986 Pamela Sargent, *Venus of Dreams*, the first of her Venus trilogy
1987 Octavia E. Butler's *Dawn*, the first of her Xenogenesis trilogy; K.W. Jeter coins 'steampunk'
1989 David Wingrove, *The Middle Kingdom*
1990 William Gibson and Bruce Sterling, *The Difference Engine*; first Web-server launched at start of World-Wide Web by Tim Berners-Lee
1992 Kim Stanley Robinson, *Red Mars*; Connie Willis, *Doomsday Book*
1993 Vernor Vinge proposes the Technological Singularity; Harold Ramis's film *Groundhog Day*
1994 Greg Egan's *Permutation City* considers a simulated universe; Catherine Asaro, 'Light and Shadow', start of the Saga of the Skolian Empire
1999 Alan Moore, *The League of Extraordinary Gentlemen*

2001 Alastair Reynolds, *Chasm City*
2003 Charles Stross, *Singularity Sky*
2005 Geoff Ryman, *Air*, looks at a non-cyber internet
2006 Vernor Vinge, *Rainbow's End*
2007 Liu Cixin, *San Ti*, the first of his Three Bodies trilogy; Rudy Rucker, *Postsingular*;
2009 China Miéville, *The City & The City*

Further Information

Further Reading

Aldiss, Brian W. and Wingrove, David, *Trillion Year Spree* (London: Victor Gollancz, 1986)

Alkon, Paul K., *Origins of Futuristic Fiction* (Athens, GA: University of Georgia Press, 1987)

Alkon, Paul K., *Science Fiction Before 1900* (New York: Twayne, 1994)

Andrews, Stephen E. and Rennison, Nick, *100 Must-Read Science Fiction Novels* (London: A. & C. Black, 2006)

Ashley, Mike, *The Time Machines* (Liverpool: Liverpool University Press, 2000)

Ashley, Mike, *Transformations* (Liverpool: Liverpool University Press, 2005)

Ashley, Mike, *Gateways to Forever* (Liverpool: Liverpool University Press, 2007)

Ashley, Mike and Lowndes, Robert A.W., *The Gernsback Days* (Holicong, PA: Wildside Press, 2004)

Bailey, J.O. *Pilgrims Through Space and Time* (New York: Argus Books, 1947)

Bell, Andrew L. and Molina-Gavilán, Yolanda (editors), *Cosmos Latinos* (Middletown, CT: Wesleyan University Press, 2003)

Bleiler, Everett F. with Bleiler, Richard J., *Science Fiction: The Early Years* (Kent, OH: Kent State University Press, 1990)

Bleiler, Everett F. with Bleiler, Richard J., *Science Fiction: The Gernsback Years* (Kent, OH: Kent State University Press, 1998)

Bly, Robert W., *The Science in Science Fiction* (Dallas, TX: Benbella Books, 2005)

Bould, Mark, Butler, Andrew M., Roberts, Adam and Vint, Sherryl (editors), *Fifty Key Figures in Science Fiction* (Abingdon: Routledge, 2010)

Brake, Professor Mark L. and Hook, Reverend Neil, *Different Engines: How Science Drives Fiction and Fiction Drives Science* (Basingstoke: Macmillan, 2008)

Clareson, Thomas D., *Science Fiction in America, 1870s–1930s* (Westport, CT: Greenwood Press, 1984)

Clarke, I.F., *The Tale of the Future* (London: The Library Association, 1961)

Clarke, I.F., *The Pattern of Expectation, 1644–2001* (London: Jonathan Cape, 1979)

Clarke, I.F., (editor), *The Tale of the Next Great War* (Liverpool, Liverpool University Press, 1995)

Clute, John and Nicholls, Peter (editors), *The Encyclopedia of Science Fiction* (London: Orbit, 1993)

D'Ammassa, Don, *Encyclopedia of Science Fiction* (New York: Facts on File, 2005)

Di Fate, Vincent, *Infinite Worlds: The Fantastic Visions of Science Fiction Art* (London: Virgin Books, 1997)

Donawerth, Jane L. and Kolmerten, Carol A. (editors), *Utopian and Science Fiction by Women: Worlds of Difference* (Liverpool: Liverpool University Press, 1994)

Frank, Jane, *A Biographical Dictionary of Science Fiction and Fantasy Artists of the Twentieth Century* (Jefferson, NC: McFarland, 2009)

Fetzer, Leland, *Pre-Revolutionary Russian Science Fiction* (Ann Arbor, MI: 1982)

Frewin, Anthony, *One Hundred Years of Science Fiction Illustration* (London: Jupiter Books, 1974)

Gunn, James, *The Science of Science-Fiction Writing* (Lanham, MD: Scarecrow Press, 2003)

Gunn, James and Candelaria, Matthew, *Speculations on Speculation* (Lanham, MD: Scarecrow Press, 2005)

James, Edward and Mendlesohn, Farah, *The Cambridge Companion to Science Fiction* (Cambridge: Cambridge University Press, 2003)

Kyle, David, *The Illustrated Book of Science Fiction Ideas & Dreams* (London: Hamlyn, 1977)

Kyle, David, *A Pictorial History of Science Fiction* (London: Hamlyn, 1976)

Larbalestier, Justin, (editor), *Daughters of Earth: Feminist Science Fiction in the Twentieth Century* (Middletown, CT: Wesleyan University Press, 2006)

Lewis, Jr., Arthur O., *Utopian Literature: American Utopias* (New York: Arno Press, 1971)

Luckhurst, Roger, *Science Fiction* (Cambridge: Polity Press, 2005)

Lundwall, Sam J., *Science Fiction: What's It All About* (New York: Ace Books, 1971)

Moskowitz, Sam (editor), *The Crystal Man* (Garden City, NY: Doubleday, 1973)

Moskowitz, Sam, *Explorers of the Infinite* (Cleveland: World Publishing, 1963)

Moskowitz, Sam, *Seekers of Tomorrow* (Cleveland: World Publishing, 1966)

Moskowitz, Sam, *Strange Horizons, The Spectrum of Science Fiction* (New York: Charles Scribner's, 1976)

Pringle, David, *The Ultimate Guide to Science Fiction* (London: Grafton, 1990)

Roberts, Adam, *The History of Science Fiction* (Basingstoke: Palgrave Macmillan, 2005)

Robinson, Frank M., *Science Fiction of the 20th Century* (Portland, OR: Collectors Press, 1999)

Rottensteiner, Franz, *The Science Fiction Book* (London: Thames and Hudson, 1975)

Rottensteiner, Franz (editor), *The Black Mirror & Other Stories* (Middletown, CT: Wesleyan University Press, 2008)

Rottensteiner, Franz (editor), *View from Another Shore*, revised edition (Liverpool: Liverpool University Press, 1999)

Seed, David, *Anticipations, Essays on Early Science Fiction and its Precursors* (Liverpool: Liverpool University Press, 1995)

Stableford, Brian, *Historical Dictionary of Science Fiction Literature* (Lanham, MD: Scarecrow Press, 2004)

Stableford, Brian, *Opening Minds* (Rockville, MD: Wildside/Borgo Press, 1995)

Stableford, Brian, *Science Fact and Science Fiction* (Abingdon: Routledge, 2006)

Stableford, Brian, *Scientific Romance in Britain, 1890–1950* (London: Fourth Estate, 1985)

Stableford, Brian (editor), *The Germans on Venus* (Encino, CA: Black Coat Press, 2009)

Stableford, Brian (editor), *News from the Moon* (Encino, CA: Black Coat Press, 2007)

Staicar, Tom, *The Feminine Eye: Science Fiction and the Women Who Write It* (New York: Frederick Ungar, 1982)

Sutherland, John, *The Longman Companion to Victorian Fiction*, second edition (London: Pearson, 2009)

Suvin, Darko, *Victorian Science Fiction in the UK* (Boston: G.K. Hall, 1983)

Westfahl, Gary, *The Mechanics of Wonder* (Liverpool: Liverpool University Press, 1998)

Westfahl, Gary, *Space and Beyond: The Frontier Theme in Science Fiction* (Westport, CT: Greenwood Press, 2000)

Wu Dingbo and Murphy, Patrick D., *Science Fiction from China* (Westport, CT: Praeger, 1989)

Websites

http://www.analogsf.com/2011_01-02/index. shtml '*Analog Science Fiction and Fact*', oldest surviving science fiction magazine, founded 1930, edited by Stanley Schmidt.

http://www.asimovs.com/2011_01/index. shtml '*Asimov's Science Fiction Magazine*', founded 1977, edited by Sheila Williams.

http://www.bsfa.co.uk 'The British Science Fiction Association', founded 1958.

http://clarkesworldmagazine.com/ '*Clarkesworld*', science fiction and fantasy magazine, edited by Neil Clarke.

http://extrapolation.utb.edu/ '*Extrapolation*', magazine of critical essays and reviews, founded 1959.

http://www.fantasticfiction.co.uk/ 'Fantastic Fiction', compiled by David Wands.

http://ttapress.com/interzone/ '*Interzone*', Britain's science fiction and fantasy magazine, founded 1982. Published by Andy Cox.

http://io9.com/ 'IO9: We Come from the Future', edited by Annalee Newitz and Charlie Jane Sanders.

http://www.isfdb.org/cgi-bin/index.cgi 'Internet Speculative Fiction Database', compiled by Al von Ruff.

http://www.locusmag.com/ 'Locus Online: The Magazine of the Science Fiction & Fantasy Field'.

http://www.wsu.edu/~brians/nuclear/index. htm 'Nuclear Holocausts: Atomic War in Fiction', by Paul Brians.

http://www.sf-foundation.org/ 'Science Fiction Foundation', Liverpool University, founded 1970.

http://www.sfra.org/ 'Science Fiction Research Organisation', founded 1970.

http://sfscope.com/ 'SF Scope', news and review magazine, edited by Ian Randal Strock

http://www.sfsignal.com/ 'SF Signal' review and news magazine, edited by John DeNardo.

http://www.sfsite.com/ 'SF Site: the Home Page for Science Fiction and Fantasy', editor Rodger Turner.

http://www.depauw.edu/sfs/ '*Science Fiction Studies*', magazine of critical essays, founded 1973.

http://www.sffworld.com/about.html 'SFF World', news and reviews, run by Dag Rambraut

http://www.strangehorizons.com/WhoWeAre. shtml 'Strange Horizons', weekly magazine of science fiction, edited by Susan Marie Groppi

http://www.uchronia.net/ 'Uchronia, the Alternate Histories List', by Robert B. Schmunk.

http://www.magicdragon.com/UltimateSF/ SF-Index.html 'The Ultimate Science Fiction Web Guide', run by Jonathan Post.

http://www.trin.cam.ac.uk/rws1001/utopia/ default.htm 'Utopian Writing, 1516–1798', by Dr Clare Jackson and Dr Richard Serjeantson

http://worldsf.wordpress.com/ 'The World SF Blog', run by Lavie Tidhar

http://www.bibliotecapleyades.net/vida_alien/ xenology/contents.htm 'Xenology: An Introduction to the Scientific Study of Extraterrestrial Life, Intelligence and Civilization', by Robert A. Freitas, Jr.

Index

Pages listed in **bold** refer to an author feature and pages in *italics* to an illustration.